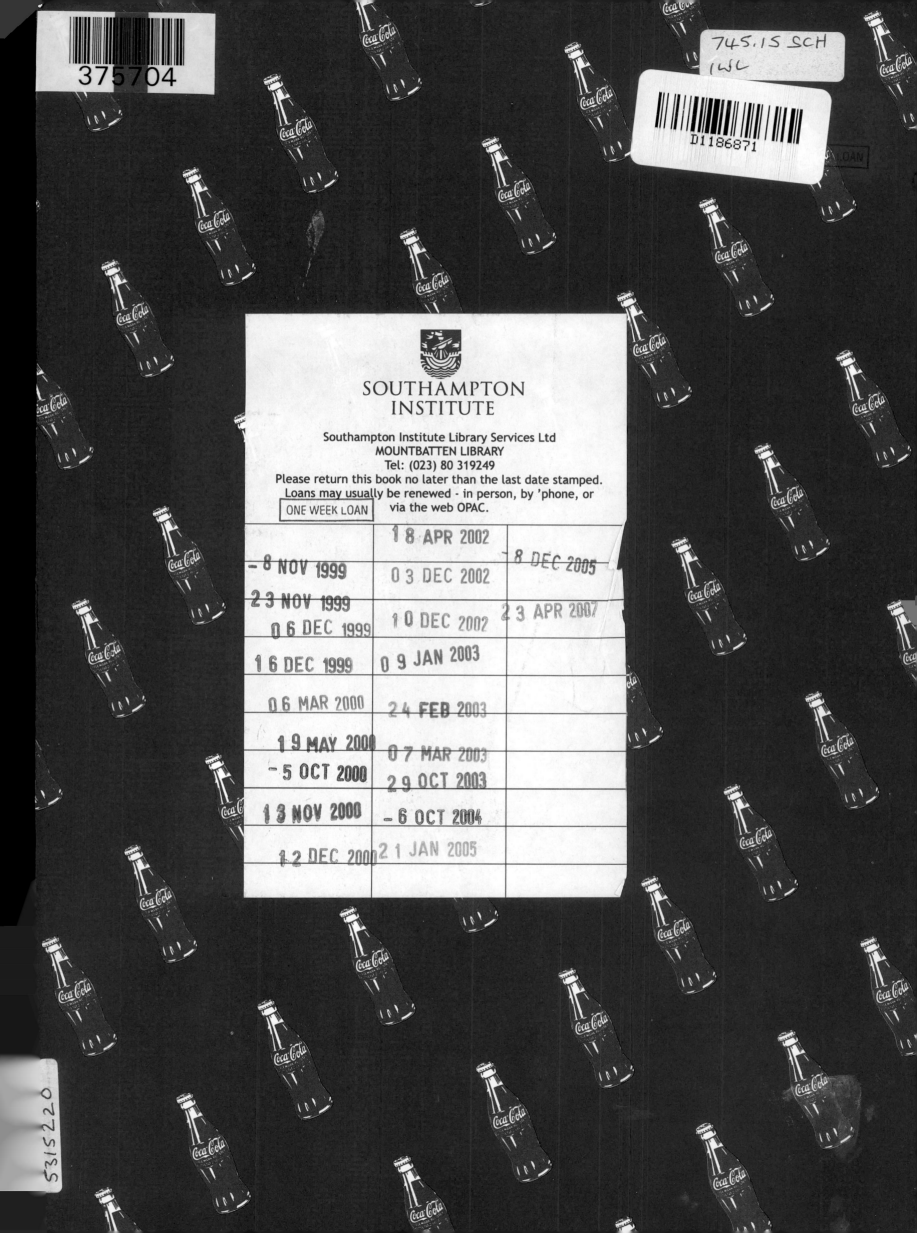

COCA-COLA

COCA-COLA

A COLLECTOR'S GUIDE TO NEW AND VINTAGE COCA-COLA MEMORABILIA

Randy Schaeffer and Bill Bateman

APPLE

Dedicated to our parents
Evelyn A. and William H. Bateman
and
Lucille C. and Stewart E. Schaeffer

A QUINTET BOOK

Published by The Apple Press
6 Blundell Street
London N7 9BH

Reprinted 1996, 1997

ISBN 1-85076-561-8

This book was designed and produced by
Quintet Publishing Limited
6 Blundell Street
London N7 9BH

Creative Director: Richard Dewing
Designer: Ian Hunt
Senior Editor: Laura Sandelson
Editor: Maggie McCormick
Photographer: Ian Howes

Typeset in Great Britain by
Central Southern Typesetters, Eastbourne
Manufactured in Singapore by Bright Arts Pte Ltd
Printed in China

All of the items shown in this book come from the
William E. Bateman and Randy S. Schaeffer
collection.

The authors assume full responsibility for facts and
information contained in this book. All opinions
expressed are those of the authors and not of
The Coca-Coca Company.

"Coca-Cola" and "Coke" are registered trade marks
which identify the same product of The Coca-Cola
Company.

CONTENTS

INTRODUCTION

For more than a century, Coca-Cola has been an integral part of American life. From its humble beginnings in 1886 in Atlanta, Georgia, to its current status as the world's pre-eminent soft drink, Coca-Cola has been heavily advertised using virtually every trick in the ad-man's repertoire. Long before today's mass media, The Coca-Cola Company used millions of promotional items to advertise and sell their product to the masses. These items ranged from utilitarian merchandising items such as bottles and cooler boxes to traditional and familiar advertising items such as signs and print advertisements; from point-of-purchase items such as trays and calendars to complimentary novelties such as toys and bookmarks.

These items form the basis for today's collections of Coca-Cola memorabilia. Part of the charm of these items for the collector is that their original purpose was to promote the sale of Coca-Cola, not to be collected. Naturally, many of the older items have not survived for today's collectors. Hence, rarity plays a role in the evaluation of Coca-Cola collectibles. Another element is the condition of the material that has survived. A third factor used to evaluate Coca-Cola collectibles is the desirability of the items themselves. For example, objects that show pictorial artwork are usually more highly prized than those that do not.

Unlike other collecting areas that may be somewhat one-dimensional, Coca-Cola collectibles literally span the full range of artifacts manufactured to merchandise and advertise consumer products since the 1880s. In retrospect, The Coca-Cola Company was not a merchandising and advertising genius. It simply merchandised and advertised by all means available, keeping the things that worked and eliminating those that did not. Its wisdom was the foresight to advertise Coca-Cola aggressively, even when profits were small and the market was soft.

LEFT **Cardboard sign, 1901, 20 cm (8-inch) diameter. This sign, complete with brass frame and chain for hanging, shows stage actress Hilda Clark. This artwork is called "Hilda Clark with the Roses".**

RIGHT **Metal tray, 1900, 24 cm (9⅝ inch-) diameter. Featuring Hilda Clark, this tray has a border decorated with cola nuts and coca leaves. Because four different poses of Hilda Clark were used for Coca-Cola advertising, this one has been named "Hilda Clark with a Glass" to distinguish it from the other three.**

ABOVE **Trade card, 1894, 10 × 14 cm (3⅞ × 5⅜ inches). Usually larger than business cards, trade cards were distributed to** **prospective customers by company salesmen. The reverse side of this example carries sales figures for 1892 and 1893.**

In addition to the wide variety and great numbers of articles produced, there are two more reasons why so many Coca-Cola items have survived. The articles used to advertise Coca-Cola were usually made of the best-quality materials. For example, it cost The Coca-Cola Company £3,333 ($5,000) just for the dies needed to produce a self-framed metal sign featuring "Betty", the Coca-Cola girl for 1914. The attractiveness of these items also accounts in part for the high survival rate, since many people saved these items at the time. The result for the collector is a rich variety of memorabilia unparalleled by any other consumer product.

In the area of "antique advertising", Coca-Cola items are regarded as the premier collectibles and invariably command the highest prices.

ABOVE **Metal sign, 1914, 78 × 104 cm (30¾ × 41 inches). One of the largest metal Coca-Cola signs for indoor use, this self-framed sign was manufactured by the Passaic** **Metal Ware Company. The same "Betty" artwork was used on the trays and calendars for 1914.**

The considerable interest in collecting older items has created a secondary level of new collectible items especially for sale to collectors as well as to the general public. At first The Coca-Cola Company discouraged such efforts, but now through licensing agreements with various manufacturers, the Company helps to identify images and items that may be produced. New items using old artwork fall into two categories: those that closely imitate old material are called reproductions, and those that do not are called fantasy items. Since many of these new things appear older than they actually are, collectors not only have to be knowledgeable about older items, but also about reproduction and fantasy lines.

As The Coca-Cola Company expanded its activities to more than 195 countries around the world, it has individualized the advertising approach to the countries in which Coca-Cola is sold. The result has been a whole new class of collectibles, with the Coca-Cola advertising appearing in a multitude of non-English languages. Not only are the many languages distinctive, but the pieces themselves are often unique to a specific country. Such items are especially prized when the artwork reflects the culture of the native country, rather than merely being an imitation of advertising used in the United States. No matter what country they hail from, most Coca-Cola collectors eagerly add foreign Coca-Cola items to their collections when they have the opportunity. For many, part of the excitement of finding foreign items comes from being part of a collecting hobby that is not limited by international borders.

Although it has become an international product, Coca-Cola is regarded worldwide as the quintessential icon of American life. Coca-Cola collectibles hold a mirror to America's past and present: its customs, values, tastes, obsessions, pleasures and troubles. For many people, collecting the advertising in use when they were growing up allows them to recapture simpler times. For others, the advertising of Coca-Cola exemplifies the American dream of a better way of life.

RIGHT **Cardboard cutout, 1929, 79 cm (31 inches) wide. This sign is the centrepiece of the five-piece "Nasturtium" festoon, which would have been used to decorate the backbar of a soda fountain.**

BELOW RIGHT **Cardboard sign, 1933, 26 × 50 cm (10¼ × 19¾ inches). During the 1930s, signs such as this one were used to promote drinking Coca-Cola at mealtimes. Called a hanger, this sign is die-cut and folded, thereby giving it a three-dimensional effect.**

RIGHT **Cardboard cutout, 1926, 46 cm (18 inches) high. The boy vendor shown in this artwork would have been a familiar sight at ballparks in the 1920s. It was also produced in a nearly life-sized version.**

ABOVE **Paper poster, 1947, 41 ×** United States, the language is
69 cm (16 × 27 inches). Although Dutch, indicating that it was
this sign was printed in the for export to the Netherlands.

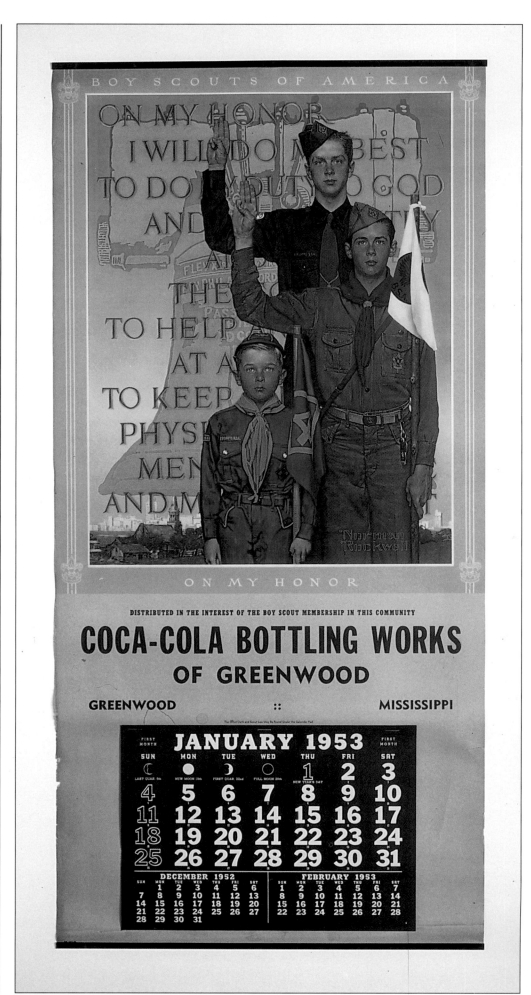

LEFT **Calendar, 1953, 41 × 84 cm (16 × 33 inches). One of a series of Boy Scout calendars illustrated by Norman Rockwell, this calendar was distributed by the Greenwood, Mississippi, Coca-Cola bottler.**

ABOVE **Disc, 1942, 23 cm (9-inch) diameter. Manufactured by the Permanent Sign & Display Company of Reading, Pennsylvania, this sign was made by covering a metal disc with paper on which the advertising had been printed. For durability, the sign was covered with plastic.**

THE HISTORY OF COCA-COLA

CHAPTER

1886 TO WORLD WAR I

Dr John S Pemberton is said to have first concocted Coca-Cola in the spring of 1886. Prior to that time, he had marketed many different products, one of which was called "French Wine Coca", because of its two main components, Bordeaux wine and extract of coca. By 1886, in an apparent effort to get on the then-popular anti-alcohol temperance bandwagon, Pemberton decided to make a non-alcoholic product based on French Wine Coca by eliminating the wine. To help mask the relatively unpleasant taste of this mixture of coca and kola, he added several aromatic oils and spices: lemon, orange, vanilla, nutmeg, coriander, cinnamon, etc. The resultant product was then sold as an over-the-counter medicine to be taken "a teaspoonful in a glass of water".

By 1887, Pemberton apparently had decided that carbonated water was the mixer to use. The label for "Coca-Cola Syrup and Extract" that he sent to the US Patent Office stated that Coca-Cola was "dispensed from the soda water fountain or in other carbonated beverages". Credit for the name "Coca-Cola" is usually given to Frank M Robinson, secretary of the Pemberton Chemical Company. By changing the "k" in kola to a "c", Robinson created a name that was both pleasant to the ear and, more importantly, one that followed the commonplace practice of using alliterative names for products in the drug trade. Robinson is also credited with designing the distinctive script form of the name. Coca-Cola in block letters appeared as early as 29 May, 1886, in an advertisement in *The Daily Journal,* an Atlanta newspaper; and script Coca-Cola was used as early as 16 June, 1887, in another advertisement for the product in the same newspaper.

LEFT **Celluloid bookmark, 1896,
6 × 7 cm (2⅜ × 2¾ inches). Made
of celluloid (a forerunner of
plastic), this bookmark was the
first in a series of heart-shaped
bookmarks. The centre portion
had a slit so that it could be
slipped over a page.**

Whether because of failing health, a need to raise capital or lack of confidence in Coca-Cola, Pemberton began selling his interest in Coca-Cola during the summer of 1887. Asa G Candler, a fellow druggist, was interested in Coca-Cola because he had tried it for his persistent headaches and "was relieved", not once, but on several occasions. As a druggist, Candler would have found headache relief significant since the pain-relieving properties of aspirin were not discovered until a dozen years later. Through a series of transactions, Candler gained total control of Coca-Cola by the end of the summer of 1888 for an investment of just over £1,533 ($2,300). Candler immediately did two things: he hired Robinson as general superintendent, and he changed the formula so that Coca-Cola syrup would be more uniform, chemically stable and better tasting.

Because sales of Coca-Cola had increased from 95 *l* (25 gallons) in 1886 to a phenomenal 33,500 *l* (8,855 gallons) in 1890, Candler divested himself of his wholesale and retail drug business's inventory in order to concentrate on promoting Coca-Cola (as well as two other products: De-lec-ta-lave, "a tooth whitener and hardener", and Botanic Blood Balm, "a cure for all blood and skin diseases"). Collectibles from this time period are extremely rare. Virtually the only items available to collectors are letters written by Pemberton, Candler and others on stationery imprinted with "Coca-Cola". These letters are even more valuable when the correspondence discusses the business of selling Coca-Cola.

ABOVE **Paper label, 1885, 5 × 10 cm (2 × 3⅞ inches). In addition to coca and wine, Pemberton's French Wine Coca also contained kola nut extract, recognized as a headache cure and hangover remedy because of its caffeine content. Bottles of the product were packaged in boxes with this label.**

BELOW **Spoon, c. 1895, 15 cm (6 inches) long. With its embossed bowl, this silver-plated spoon was used to mix the finished product in a glass after Coca-Cola syrup and carbonated water had been added individually.**

ABOVE **Letterhead, 1907, 22 cm (8⅜ inches) wide. After starting in Atlanta, The Coca-Cola Company soon had branches scattered throughout the United States, Canada, and Cuba, as shown on this elaborate letterhead.**

LEFT **Trade card, 1891, 13 × 10 cm (4⅞ × 3¾ inches). The reverse side of this trade card carries sales figures for Coca-Cola in the city of Atlanta for the year 1890. At that time, Coca-Cola was still being advertised more as a medicinal product than a soft drink.**

On 13 April, 1891, Candler became the "sole proprietor" of Coca-Cola. Candler incorporated the business the following year, and a charter was granted to "The Coca-Cola Company", a Georgia corporation, on 29 January, 1892. Candler turned over to the new corporation all his personal rights to Coca-Cola in exchange for half the stock in the new company. By 1895, Candler was able to report that "Coca-Cola is now sold and drunk in every state and territory in the United States". The missionary zeal of Asa Candler was apparent in his 1896 report to the stockholders when he stated, "We have not lagged in our efforts to go into all the world, teaching that Coca-Cola is the article, par excellence, for the health and good feeling of all the people". The 1890s would see the first expansion of syrup-making facilities to locations outside Atlanta: Dallas in 1894, Chicago by 1897, Philadelphia and Los Angeles in 1898. It was also during the 1890s that bottling of the finished product (Coca-Cola plus carbonated water) began – first by Joseph Biedenharn in Vicksburg, Mississippi, in 1894; and second by Holmes & Barber in Valdosta, Georgia, in 1897. The bottling of Coca-Cola did not really achieve official status until 1899, when

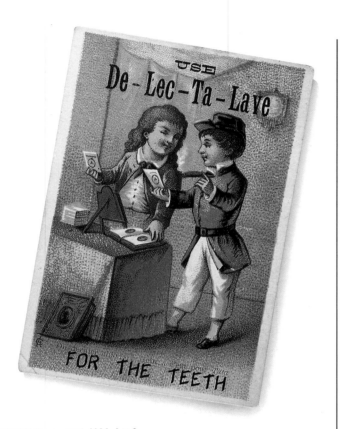

ABOVE **Trade card, 1886, 6 × 9 cm (2½ × 3⅝ inches). De-lec-ta-lave, a liquid dentifrice, was purchased by Asa Candler from** **Dr Brockett for £2,500 ($3,750), more than one and a half times what he paid for Coca-Cola.**

ABOVE **Cardboard fan, c. 1893, 22 × 30 cm (8½ × 12⅛ inches). In 1892, Candler granted the distribution rights for Coca-Cola in New England to Seth W Fowle, a Boston wholesaler, who held the rights for twenty years. This fan is just one of many examples of local advertising for Coca-Cola.**

Benjamin Thomas and Joseph Whitehead persuaded Asa Candler to sign a contract on 21 July, 1899, giving them exclusive rights to bottle Coca-Cola in most of the country (except for Mississippi, Texas and the New England states). Whitehead soon sold half his interest to Joseph Lupton, a Chattanooga lawyer, for £1,666 ($2,500) in order to have the necessary capital to begin bottling Coca-Cola. A system of syrup wholesalers, called "parent bottlers", was established to act as middlemen between The Coca-Cola Company, which made the syrup, and the local bottlers who actually packaged the finished product in bottles throughout the country.

From its very beginning, Coca-Cola was advertised heavily. The philosophy for this marketing approach appears in the 7 December, 1892, First Annual Stockholders Report of the President of The Coca-Cola Company. Candler stated: "We have done very considerable advertising in territory which has not yet yielded any returns. We have reason to believe that it will

LEFT **Ceramic syrup urn, c. 1900, 46 cm (18 inches) high. The upper portion of this three-piece unit held approximately 4 l (one** **gallon) of Coca-Cola syrup. A spigot on the reverse side was used to dispense the syrup directly into a glass.**

show good returns during the ensuing year. In all territory developed previous to the incorporation of the Company, there has been a very large increase of business compared to former years." From the fact that they made annual percentage comparisons between the increased amount spent for advertising and the increased sales of Coca-Cola, it is clear that the Company's officers well understood the connection between advertising and sales. Pre-1900 Coca-Cola collectibles include stationery, booklets, postcards, trade cards, free-drink coupons, calendars, bookmarks, trays, clocks, syrup urns, fans, napkins, canvas banners, paper and cardboard posters and metal signs.

The decade from 1901 to 1910 saw a continued increase in sales from 5,000 *l* (1,300 gallons) to 43,500 *l* (11,500 gallons) a day and an increase from £66,666 ($100,000) spent on advertising in 1901 to £566,666 ($850,000) in 1910. Coca-Cola was first advertised in national consumer magazines in the summer of 1904, although previously there had been advertising in some drug and religious publications. In 1906, The Coca-Cola Company proclaimed to its retailers: "We are doing some of the handsomest and most artistic advertising ever done in this country or any other country. We are spending thousands of dollars in telling people to go to your store for Coca-Cola". From the late 1890s into the 1910s, Wolf & Company, a Philadelphia-based advertising agency, arranged for much of the advertising for Coca-Cola. In a biography of his father, Asa Candler's son said, "It was always one of the high spots of the year when Mr David Wolf would drive up . . . with several large portfolios containing proofs of the calendars and hangers for next season". The Massengale Agency was responsible for placing advertisements for Coca-Cola in magazines in the early part of this century. William C D'Arcy was selected in 1906 to help place advertising in daily papers, trade publications and streetcars. By the end of the decade, the D'Arcy Advertising Company was handling more than one quarter of the Company's advertising budget. Many collectors know D'Arcy because he originated the "Whenever you see an arrow, think of Coca-Cola" campaign.

LEFT **Free-drink coupon, letter and envelope, c. 1895. As a means of promoting Coca-Cola, the Company mailed coupons for free drinks to potential customers from lists supplied by local soda-fountain operators. This marketing strategy was largely responsible for the early success of Coca-Cola.**

ABOVE **Sheet music, 1906, 26 × 34 cm (10¼ × 13¼ inches).** *Juanita* **was one of ten different songs available as sheet music from The Coca-Cola Company. Lithographed in Germany, the** cover of this sheet music used the same artwork as the 1906 trays and calendars. Because of the association with this particular song, this artwork is commonly called "Juanita".

ABOVE **Magazine advertisement, 1909, 22 × 28 cm (8⅜ × 10⅞ inches). Appearing in the 20 May, 1909, issue of** *Life* **magazine, this advertisement was one of many placed by the D'Arcy agency which incorporated arrows in the artwork. The arrows were to "point the way" to refreshment.**

RIGHT **Trade card,** *c.* **1907, 16 × 9 cm (6¼ × 3½ inches) folded (closed, open and rear views shown). Issued by the Chicago-based Western Coca-Cola Bottling Company, a parent bottler, this amusing metamorphic "Bathtub" trade card opens to reveal that the woman's knees are actually the heads of men being served Coca-Cola.**

ABOVE **Postcard, 1910, 9 × 14 cm (3⅜ × 5½ inches). This "Motor Girl" artwork is also called "Duster Girl" because the** woman is wearing the typical "duster" coat worn by early motorists to ward off the effects of dirt roads. Designed to promote Coca-Cola in bottles, this artwork also appears on such other advertising items as watch fobs, match safes, pocket mirrors, calendars and posters.

RIGHT **Photograph, 1909, 19 × 24 cm (7⅝ × 9½ inches). Taken at the 1909 New Jersey Fair, this photograph shows the award-winning Coca-Cola booth. Close examination reveals dozens of Coca-Cola advertising items including signs, trays, posters, cutouts, bottles, openers, glasses, 24-bottle cases, fans and thermometers.**

LEFT **Cardboard fan, c. 1915, 34 × 20 cm (13⅜ × 8 inches). Chewing gum flavoured with Coca-Cola was produced from 1903 to the early 1920s, first by the Coca-Cola Chewing Gum Company in Atlanta and later by the Franklin Caro Company in Richmond, Virginia. The reverse side of this fan shows scenes of Richmond, the "Home of Coca-Cola Gum".**

RIGHT **Syrup jug, c. 1912, 30 cm (11¾ inches) high. As the popularity of Coca-Cola spread throughout the country, the syrup was shipped in containers such as this 4 l (one-gallon) earthenware jug. At one ounce per serving, 4 l (one gallon) served 128 customers.**

CONCERNING OUR RESTRICTED OUTPUT

We have made our sacrifice for war, and are cheerfully complying with the regulations of the Food Administration. For you to accept a substitute for Coca-Cola is to defeat the purpose of the Government for the conservation of sugar.

THE COCA-COLA COMPANY

Sugar is a war essential.. .....Save it!

LEFT **Cardboard streetcar sign, 1918, 53 × 28 cm (21 × 11 inches). Because of sugar rationing during World War I, The Coca-Cola Company was forced to restrict its production. In an obvious appeal to patriotism, this sign shows the silhouette of the Statue of Liberty's torch as the shadow of a hand holding a glass of Coca-Cola.**

The independently owned bottling business also thrived, and by the end of the decade in 1910, local bottlers were using over 30% of all the syrup produced. Increasingly, advertising depicted Coca-Cola in bottles, and the use of advertising novelties increased exponentially. Advertising expenditures listed in Company records during this time included giveaways such as wallets, coin purses, pocket mirrors, matches, pocketknives, watch fobs, blotters, pencils and fans.

With its great financial success, The Coca-Cola Company was the target of imitators, dubbed the "Pirates of Business" in one of the Company's newspaper advertisements. Company lawyers were kept busy prosecuting the likes of the Koke Company, Karo-Cola, Curo-Cola, Sola Cola, Koca-Nola, and Taka-Kola for trademark infringement. Some Coca-Cola collectors regularly collect the advertising of the imitators as well, but the value of such collectibles, with the exception of a few early Pepsi-Cola items, is minimal in comparison to Coca-Cola collectibles. With the passage of the Pure Food and Drug Act in 1906, the legal woes of the Company were further compounded as Coca-Cola also became the target of US federal government litigation concerning its contents, especially caffeine.

Sales of Coca-Cola steadily increased in volume from 1886 to 1917. In 1917, however, the United States found itself involved in World War I. Many staples were rationed, most notably sugar, one of the two main ingredients of Coca-Cola (the other being water). These conditions forced the Company to curtail the production of syrup. Advertising was kept to a minimum, since there was obviously no point in advertising a product with limited supply. Coca-Cola sales dropped from 15 million *l* (12 million gallons) in 1917 to 38 million *l* (10 million gallons) in 1918 – the first drop in the history of Coca-Cola. With the end of the war, restrictions eased, sugar became available again, advertising increased and sales rebounded to almost 72 million *l* (19 million gallons) in 1919. As a magazine advertisement so proudly declared, "Victory's Reward Means Volume Restored".

BETWEEN THE WARS

The period immediately following World War I was unsettled financially and legally for The Coca-Cola Company. The price of sugar continued to fluctuate and with it the financial condition of the Company. The trademark infringement case brought against the Koke Company in 1912 had yet to be settled in 1919 when a consortium of banks made an offer of £16.6 million ($25 million) to purchase The Coca-Cola Company. Fearing the loss of their most valuable asset, the Coca-Cola trademark, and perhaps tiring of the seemingly endless lawsuits with imitators and the federal government, the major stockholders accepted the offer. The privately held business which had been a Georgia corporation was re-incorporated as a publicly held Delaware corporation, but the name, The Coca-Cola Company, stayed the same.

The Koke Company case was finally resolved in The Coca-Cola Company's favour in 1920 with a decree handed down by the US Supreme Court. Written by Associate Justice Oliver Wendell Holmes, this ruling recognized that Koke was indeed a popular abbreviation for Coca-Cola; that the Koke Company had illegally taken advantage of this fact; and, last and most importantly, that Coca-Cola meant "a single thing from a single source, and well known to the community". Although imitations would continue to plague The Coca-Cola Company, this

ABOVE **Cardboard hanger, c. 1915, 18 cm (7 inches) square. Of all the imitations that took advantage of the popularity of** Coca-Cola, none was as serious a threat to the Coca-Cola trade-mark as was Koke, the logo for which imitated that for Coca-Cola.

landmark decision in trademark law established the validity and strength of the Coca-Cola trademark.

Although sales rebounded after the war to an all-time high in 1919, business decreased in 1920, 1921 and 1922. The new owners of the Company became justifiably concerned and on 28 April, 1923, elected Robert W Woodruff president of the Company. Robert was the son of Ernest Woodruff, the man who had masterminded the takeover of the Company in 1919. As one of his first acts as president, Woodruff established a separate department called Quality Control to oversee all phases in the

LEFT **Cardboard box, 1927, 10 × 7 cm (3¾ × 2¾ inches). In 1927, The Coca-Cola Company granted the Startup Candy Company of Provo, Utah, a license to manufacture "chocolate pellets filled with Coca-Cola syrup". The box shown here held two ounces of candy and cost 6p (10¢).**

preparation of the finished product: from seeing that the carbonated water used locally was of sufficient purity to seeing that the right bottle caps were used. Woodruff also re-organized the Sales Department of the Company. He felt that salesmen should do more than take orders, that they should assist fountain operators in making the most profit from selling Coca-Cola at their fountains. He established the Fountain Sales Training School in 1926 and a year later changed the name "salesmen" to "servicemen" to better reflect the kind of job they were expected to perform. One of a serviceman's responsibilities was the proper and prominent placement of the advertising for Coca-Cola. It is said that Woodruff personally approved the artwork for such things as the annual calendars and trays. The immediate result of all these changes was that the sales of Coca-Cola showed an increase in 1923 and, indeed, every year thereafter.

If Asa Candler can be credited with making Coca-Cola a national drink, then surely Robert Woodruff deserves the credit for making Coca-Cola an international drink. While it is true that Coca-Cola had been sold outside the United States before Woodruff's presidency, it was on a relatively disorganized basis. There had been sales in Cuba, Canada, England, France, Germany and the Philippines, to name a few countries. In 1923, Woodruff established a

separate division – the Export Department, later the Foreign Department, then The Coca-Cola Export Corporation – to "take charge of [the Company's] increased activities in foreign markets". This division facilitated the establishment of bottling plants overseas, and by 1929 there were Coca-Cola bottlers in twenty-nine countries.

Two merchandising firsts occurred in the 1920s: the first six-bottle carton in 1923 and the first standardized cooler box for bottled Coca-Cola in 1929. Two new advertising media were added during the decade: 24-sheet billboards and radio programs. Many of the famous slogans associated with Coca-Cola also had their beginnings in the 1920s: "Thirst knows no season", "Enjoy thirst", "Refresh yourself", "It had to be good to get where it is", "Pure as sunlight" and "The pause that refreshes". By 1928, the sales of bottled Coca-Cola surpassed forever the fountain sales of Coca-Cola. From this point forward in the history of Coca-Cola, the amount of advertising for Coca-Cola in bottles would exceed that for Coca-Cola in glasses.

BELOW **Wooden barrel, 1939, 29 × 43 cm (11¼ × 17 inches). Beginning in the 1890s and continuing until World War II,** **large quantities of Coca-Cola syrup were shipped in wooden barrels ranging in capacity from 19 to 190 l (5 to 50 gallons).**

Keep...
Coca-Cola
IN YOUR ICE BOX

LEFT **Cardboard sign, c. 1925, 22 × 9 cm (8½ × 3½ inches). Before the popularity of six-bottle cartons, bottlers used signs such as this one to encourage people to keep bottles of Coca-Cola on ice at home. Made by the Embosograf Corporation of America in New York, this example has a construction similar to that of inlaid wood, but with cardboard instead.**

BELOW **Wooden sign, 1934, 38 × 51 cm (15 × 20 inches). The National Recovery Administration (NRA) was established in 1933 by President Franklin D Roosevelt to regulate industry and labour practices. This plywood sign was manufactured by Kay Displays, Inc., and was issued to bottlers to show their support for the programme.**

The decade of the 1930s was marked by continued growth for The Coca-Cola Company. That Coca-Cola continued to thrive during the Great Depression, while other soft drinks and businesses failed, is testimony to the nature of the product and its advertising. A parallel can be drawn to Hollywood's similar success during the 1930s – often called the Golden Age of Hollywood. That movies and the escapism they provided were so popular during this time was not lost on those in charge of the advertising for Coca-Cola. Numerous movie stars were shown, always with conspicuously present bottles and glasses of Coca-Cola, as if to say that drinking Coca-Cola would make the common person's life more glamorous. The cavalcade of stars used on Coca-Cola advertising included many of filmdom's finest: Wallace Beery, Joan Blondell, Claudette Colbert, Jackie Cooper, Joan Crawford, Clark Gable, Cary Grant, Jean Harlow, Carole Lombard, Fredric March, Maureen O'Sullivan, Johnny Weismuller and Loretta Young. Cardboard signs, cutouts and posters showing these stars are extremely popular with today's collectors.

NRA
MEMBER
US
WE DO OUR PART
Coca-Cola

Drink
Coca-Cola
Delicious and Refreshing
Tune In
31-piece Orchestra
Graham McNamee
Grantland Rice
EVERY WEDNESDAY EVENING · N.B.C. NETWORK

LEFT **Paper window strip, 1930, 68 × 19 cm (26¾ × 7½ inches). In 1927, a melodrama called "Vivian" was the first radio program sponsored by Coca-Cola. The second debuted in 1930 and featured sportscaster Grantland Rice interviewing celebrities of the day.**

LEFT **Paper hanger, 1932, 27 × 55 cm (10¾ × 21⅜ inches). Printed in Spanish, this sign shows Lupe Velez, affectionately called "the Mexican Spitfire", the star of many Mexican and American films during the 1930s.**

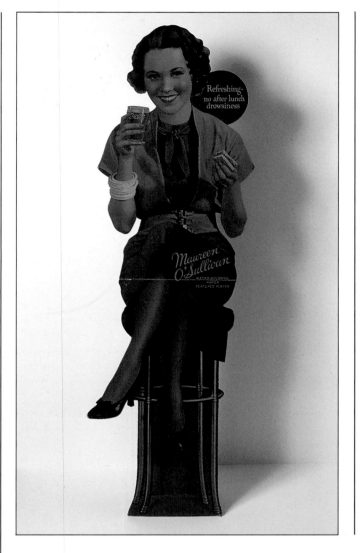

ABOVE **Cardboard cutout, 1933, 160 cm (63 inches) high. Shown here on a fountain stool and in more conventional dress, Maureen O'Sullivan is perhaps best known for playing "Jane" to Johnny Weissmuller's "Tarzan" in the films.**

ABOVE **Cardboard cutout, 1931, 51 cm (20 inches) high. Illustrator Haddon Sundblom painted his first annual Coca-Cola Santa for Christmas of 1931, a series that would extend virtually unbroken until 1964. Sundblom's Santas appear on countless cutouts, signs and posters.**

LEFT **Cardboard cutout display, 1933, 110 cm (43¼ inches) wide. The Coca-Cola Company commissioned Ida Bailey Allen, a recognized expert on food and nutrition, to write *When You Entertain*, a small book containing hospitality hints.**

ABOVE **Price lists, for 1938 and 1939, 28 × 38 cm (11 × 15 inches) closed. The Coca-Cola Company offered standardized advertising materials to the bottlers through these annual price lists. These booklets provide a wealth of information about what was produced.**

BELOW **Metal syrup can, 1940, 24 cm (9½ inches) high. The Coca-Cola Company first started shipping Coca-Cola syrup in 4 l (one-gallon) metal cans in 1939. Prior to that time, small quantities of syrup had been shipped in glass and earthenware jugs.**

ABOVE **Newspaper advertisement, 1936, 36 × 50 cm (14¼ × 19¾ inches). This full-page advertisement appeared in** the *American Weekly* section of Sunday newspapers on 14 June, 1936, in celebration of the fiftieth anniversary of Coca-Cola.

The automatic fountain dispenser for Coca-Cola developed by The Dole Valve Company of Chicago was introduced at the 1933 Chicago World's Fair. It measured out the correct amount of syrup, added carbonated water, and mixed the two together — a process that had been previously carried out by the soda-fountain clerk. The first commercially successful coin-operated cooler boxes were developed by Westinghouse in the mid-1930s. Augmenting the wooden barrels and glass jugs used to ship syrup, metal one-gallon (4 *l*) syrup cans went into production in 1939. "The Coca-Cola Radio Program" debuted in 1930; Haddon Sundblom's Coca-Cola Santas began to appear in 1931; the *When You Entertain* campaign was inaugurated in 1932; and famous illustrators — Norman Rockwell in 1931, 1932, 1934 and 1935; Frederick Stanley in 1933; and N C Wyeth in 1936 and 1937 — created the rustic artwork used on the annual calendars and other items. Coca-Cola celebrated its fiftieth anniversary in 1936 with special promotional items such as an aluminium snack bowl and advertising which

noted the anniversary. Two more radio programs sponsored by Coca-Cola debuted in the 1930s: "Refreshment Time" with Ray Noble (later with Singin' Sam instead) and "The Song Shop" with Kitty Carlisle. Although events in Europe and the Far East were ominous, the advertising used in the United States for Coca-Cola did not yet reflect it.

WORLD WAR II AND BEYOND

Naturally, the decade of the 1940s was dominated by World War II. Woodruff set the tone for the Company's operating procedure when he directed that, "We will see that every man in uniform gets a bottle of Coca-Cola for [3p] five cents wherever he is and whatever it costs". The Company carried out this pledge by building bottling plants overseas as near to the troops as possible. Company representatives were attached to the Army, and given the title "Technical Observer". By the end of the war, sixty-four bottling plants had been shipped to North Africa, Europe, Australia and the Philippines. Of more than 140 Technical Observers who saw action, three were killed in the line of duty. After the war, many of the bottling plants remained behind and were sold to local businessmen.

The war was the predominant advertising theme during this time period. Countless posters, signs, cardboard

cutouts and calendars portrayed both men and women in uniform. Displays for places of business pictured the machines of war: ships and planes. Decks of playing cards, score sheets, and even tables and chairs, all marked with the Coca-Cola logo, capitalized on the contract bridge craze that had begun in the late 1930s. Game kits, containing bingo, dominoes, draughts, darts, ping-pong, etc., were distributed to military bases both at home and abroad. The annual advertising budget swelled from £6.6 ($10) million in 1941 to £13.3 ($20) million in 1948. After the loss of a trademark infringement case against Pepsi-Cola, beginning in 1941, the trademark notification was now centred below the entire word "Coca-Cola" instead of appearing in the long trailing tail of the first "C" in "Coca" – a significant change that helps collectors date collectibles today. In 1941, the Company officially started using the nickname "Coke" as a synonymous name for Coca-Cola. Almost simultaneously in 1942, the "Sprite" was introduced, wearing a bottle cap when advertising the sales of bottled Coca-Cola and changing to a soda clerk's cap when promoting fountain sales. "Coke" was finally registered as a trademark in the United States Patent Office on 14 August, 1945.

In July 1944, the one-billionth gallon of Coca-Cola syrup was manufactured – some fifty-eight years after its beginning. The next billion gallons took only nine more years, and the third billion, six more years. It was during

ABOVE Playing cards, 1943. By showing silhouettes of Allied and Axis planes, this deck of "Spotter Cards" was meant to help servicemen abroad, as well as citizens at home, identify military aircraft. The woman on the reverse side is a US Army Nurse.

SERVICE ABOVE SELF

Be a Lifesaver — Buy War Bonds and Stamps

Armed only with courage, and dedicated to saving life and relieving pain, the men of the Medical Department go into battle. Where shells scream and bullets whine these men perform their duty. A minute saved may mean a life saved. Beside the men who fall they serve, giving first aid, quenching thirst, guarding until stretchers come. Theirs is a true devotion to mercy, a Service Above Self!

1943		October			1943	
SUNDAY	MONDAY	TUESDAY	WEDNESDAY	THURSDAY	FRIDAY	SATURDAY
					1	2
3	4	5	6	7	8	9
10	11	12	13	14	15	16
17	18	19	20	21	22	23
24 31	25	26	27	28	29	30

DELICIOUS *Coca-Cola* REFRESHING

THE COCA-COLA BOTTLING WORKS COMPANY

and Massachusetts. Collectors have diligently noted each of the above changes, not just by gathering the advertising, but by adding each variation and incarnation of the new containers to their collections.

Advertising for Coca-Cola entered the television era in 1950 with the sponsorship of a Thanksgiving Day special starring the popular ventriloquist Edgar Bergen and his dummy Charlie McCarthy. The Company's second show, a Christmas special later that year, also marked Walt

LEFT **Calendar, 1943, 48 × 100 cm (19 × 39½ inches). Through a project called "Schools at War", Coca-Cola bottlers distributed this calendar to encourage children to save their dimes for the war effort. The artwork shows a medic with a Red Cross armband giving aid to a wounded soldier on the battlefront.**

BELOW **Plastic bottle topper, 1953, 18 × 19 cm (7 × 7¼ inches). Although the Company had long fought against using nicknames for Coca-Cola, they finally relented and adopted the trademark "Coke" in the 1940s. When placed atop an ordinary bottle, this display piece reminded the public that they could use either name to get the same drink.**

DRINK *Coca-Cola* "Coke"

ASK FOR IT — EITHER WAY

WE LET YOU SEE THE BOTTLE

the 1950s that the price of a drink of Coca-Cola finally exceeded 3p (5¢). In 1955 Coca-Cola became available for the first time in sizes other than the traditional six-and-a-half-ounce bottle, and six-ounce glasses, when ten-ounce, twelve-ounce and twenty-six-ounce bottles and twelve-ounce glasses were introduced. That same year also saw the introduction of "pre-mix" vending machines that dispensed previously mixed Coca-Cola into paper cups (unlike "post-mix" machines that mix the ingredients as they are being dispensed). The flat-top can, another new container for Coca-Cola, was first used during the 1950s, but on a limited basis, initially for shipments to military bases overseas (from plants in California and Massachusetts) and later in test markets in Rhode Island

CARDBOARD CUTOUTS

BELOW **Cardboard cutout, 1958, 91 cm (35⅞ inches) high. In addition to portraying America's love affair with the automobile, this fountain sign also proclaimed the new larger glasses for Coca-Cola.**

ABOVE **Cardboard cutout, 1961, 48 cm (18¾ inches) high. The Sprite, an elfin-like creature introduced in 1942 to promote the use of the word "Coke", was called into service in the late 1950s and early 1960s to proclaim that Coca-Cola was now available in larger bottles.**

ABOVE **Paper window strip, 1949, 61 × 28 cm (24 × 11 inches). The Coca-Cola Company sponsored ventriloquist Edgar** Bergen and his dummy Charlie McCarthy on the American CBS radio network from 1949 to 1952.

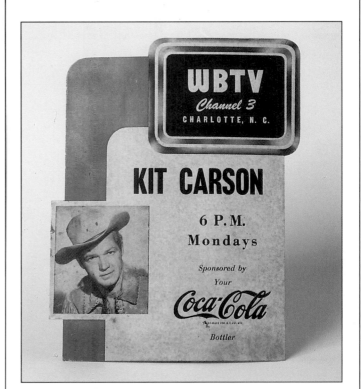

LEFT **Cardboard cutout, 1954, 48 cm (19 inches) high.** *Coke Time* with singer Eddie Fisher was a twice-weekly, fifteen-minute musical variety programme during the 1950s.

ABOVE **Cardboard cutout, c. 1953, 34 cm (13¼ inches) high.** Western frontiersman Kit Carson, as portrayed by actor Bill Williams, was immortalized in a 1950s television series sponsored by local Coca-Cola bottlers.

Disney's first entry into television. Later in the decade, Coca-Cola sponsored "Coke Time with Eddie Fisher", "The Mickey Mouse Club" and "The Adventures of Kit Carson". The Coca-Cola Company's fifty-year association with the D'Arcy Advertising Company ended in 1956, when the firm of McCann-Erickson took over the account. McCann-Erickson's first major campaign in 1957 was a series of advertisements showing people enjoying Coca-Cola in international settings. The first new logo since the bull's-eye logo had been developed in the 1930s debuted in 1958. Officially known as the "arciform" logo, nicknamed the "fishtail" logo for obvious reasons, it was soon abandoned in the early 1960s. Two of the most popular advertising items for Coca-Cola also appeared for the first time in the 1950s: the Buddy Lee doll (1950) wearing a Coca-Cola delivery man's uniform and the Santa Claus doll (1955) holding a miniature Coca-Cola bottle.

The first bottler under contract with The Coca-Cola Company began in Chattanooga in 1899 and, hence, reached its fiftieth anniversary in 1949. Dozens of other bottlers followed suit throughout the 1950s. To celebrate these fiftieth anniversaries, The Coca-Cola Company made reproductions of some early advertising items, which are occasionally mistaken today for their older counterparts.

LEFT **Doll, 1950, 33 cm (13 inches) high. To promote their products, the H D Lee Company had been marketing dolls outfitted in miniature versions of their work clothing since the early 1920s. Although Lee had manufactured uniforms for Coca-Cola employees since 1929, it wasn't until the 1950s that "Buddy Lee" dolls in Coca-Cola uniforms were sold to the general public.**

ABOVE **Metal sign, 1985, 15 × 51 cm (6 × 20 inches). This sign featuring the familiar Coca-Cola bottle with a red and white applied colour label (ACL) was made for use in Thailand. The lettering at the top above the "dynamic ribbon device" is not "Coca-Cola", but rather "Coke" in the Thai language.**

Collectors also often confuse the wealth of items manufactured in the 1950s to mark these occasions with the items made to celebrate the fiftieth anniversary of The Coca-Cola Company in 1936.

The Coca-Cola Company departed from its one-product rule for the first time in the 1950s with the introduction of the Fanta line of flavours. Sprite, TAB, Fresca and Simba followed in the 1960s. Advertising during the 1960s took on a decidedly "hip" image as popular singers such as the Supremes, Neil Diamond, Ray Charles and Aretha Franklin were recruited to promote Coca-Cola. The "things go better with Coke" logo and slogan were seen for the first time in 1963. The Company opened its own pavilion at the New York World's Fair in 1964, and special cups, postcards, matches and magazine advertisements were produced. In 1966, a new can design appeared, officially called the "harlequin" design, but more commonly known as the chequerboard design. It was short-lived, and a new slogan and logo made a grand entrance in 1969. The slogan was "It's the real thing" and the logo was the so-called "Arden Square" with the distinctive "dynamic ribbon device" appearing below the Coca-Cola trademark. The advertising throughout the next decade revolved around the "Real Thing" slogan, and the dynamic ribbon device was used on practically everything related to Coca-Cola. Not only does the dynamic ribbon device act as a dating aid, but it also serves as a convenient cutoff for many collectors who are not interested in any of the newer items produced after 1969.

ABOVE **Metal sign, 1968, 30 × 46 cm (11¾ × 18 inches).** Since the 1950s, the Company has also made a line of fruit-flavoured soft drinks called Fanta. This Spanish language sign shows the Fanta clown which was used to promote this beverage line around the world.

LEFT **Paper flyer, 1965, 30 × 20 cm (11¾ × 8 inches).** Although the Company used many popular artists to advertise Coca-Cola, the Beatles were not among them. However, the local bottler in Cleveland, Ohio, did sponsor a programme about the Beatles on a local television station.

Since that time, there have been other milestones in the history of The Coca-Cola Company, but with little impact on Coca-Cola collecting. The 1971 commercial song "I'd like to teach the world to sing . . ." was released in a non-commercial version and broke into the charts, selling well over a million copies. Probably the single most popular campaign in the entire history of Coca-Cola occurred in 1979 and featured the Pittsburgh Steelers' "Mean" Joe Greene in a heart-touching TV commercial wherein he gave his football jersey to a small boy in exchange for a drink of Coca-Cola. The 1980s spawned the creation of "megabrand" Coca-Cola comprising diet Coke, caffeine-free Coke, Cherry Coke, "new" Coke, and Classic Coca-Cola. Coca-Cola also reached another kind of high in 1985 when specially designed cans went aloft in the Space Shuttle, and Coke became the first soft drink to be drunk in space. Back on earth, space-age cans made of plastic were test-marketed by us earthbound mortals in late 1985.

Coca-Cola celebrated its hundredth anniversary in 1986. Since then, The Coca-Cola Company has continued to prosper, and so has collecting Coca-Cola memorabilia. What the second century of Coca-Cola will bring remains to be seen. One thing is for certain: Coca-Cola will be with us for a long time to come. It's difficult to imagine the world without Coca-Cola – it's been a part of our lives for as long as any of us can remember. We grew up with Coca-Cola and its wonderful advertising; we associate good times with it; and it's always been there to add some flavour to our existence. Coca-Cola collectibles allow us to pause and remember.

ABOVE **Can, 1985, 15 cm (5¾ inches) high. At a development cost of approximately £166,666 ($250,000), The Coca-Cola Company produced about 200** "Space Cans", several of which went into space aboard the Challenger Space Shuttle.

ABOVE **Paper poster, 1986, 48 × 69 cm (19 × 27¼ inches). The Coca-Cola Company celebrated the 100th anniversary of Coca-Cola during the week of 8 May,** 1986. The special logo for the Coca-Cola's Centennial Celebration in Atlanta is shown at the bottom of this poster.

GLASSES

CHAPTER 2

STRAIGHT-SIDED GLASSES

The classic Coca-Cola bottle has long been recognized as one of the most familiar objects in the world. After its introduction in the late 1910s, that bottle fairly quickly became virtually synonymous with the product. What few realize, however, is that long before that bottle came into existence, the "Coca-Cola glass" had achieved equal recognition. Until the late 1920s, the sale of fountain Coca-Cola (in glasses) far out-paced the sale of Coca-Cola in bottles. Since Coca-Cola was first concocted in 1886, most of it had been served in glasses made especially for Coca-Cola.

Consumers had come to associate the product with the glass and the glass with the product. Even glasses that were not marked "Coca-Cola" but which had the same shape were typically called "Coca-Cola glasses" by the public. Today, because Coca-Cola is available in a vast array of glasses, bottles, cups and cans, the iconic significance of the shape of the container in the early days has been largely lost. At one time, however, The Coca-Cola Company and the public alike expected, even demanded, a container they could trust. The distinctive Coca-Cola bottle is one part of the story. The distinctive glass used for Coca-Cola is the other part.

The first definitive proof of special glasses for Coca-Cola dates from 1900, when the Company began promoting a "graduated Coca-Cola glass". This glass was nothing more than a straight-sided glass to which the script Coca-Cola trademark had been added. Such glasses were known in the glass industry as "mineral water" glasses. The word "graduated" referred to the line on the glass approximately three-quarters of an inch from the bottom. Since automatic dispensing machines had not yet been invented – syrup was manually dispensed from ceramic urns and syrup bottles – this line was very important because it indicated the amount of Coca-Cola syrup to be used. Ice and carbonated water were added to fill the glass. This marking became known as the "syrup line". The size of the glass was also very important since the ratio of syrup to carbonated water had to be correct, or the finished drink would be either too strong or too weak.

LEFT **Syrup bottle, c. 1905, 30 cm (12 inches) high. Kept on the backbars of soda fountains, syrup bottles were used to store small quantities of Coca-Cola syrup until needed.**

ABOVE **Straight-sided glass and metal holder, c. 1902, 11 cm (4¼ inches) high. Straight-sided glasses in nickel silver holders appeared in Coca-Cola advertising from 1901 through** **1904. Because the glasses were easily broken and the holders were relatively expensive, very few of either have survived the passage of time.**

Clearly, in addition to advertising Coca-Cola, the glass was important for maintaining quality control – it had to be standardized. To make certain that the proper glass was available at a price that retailers could afford to use, The Coca-Cola Company purchased huge quantities of the special glasses and made them available at cost to retailers through the same distribution channels used for Coca-Cola syrup.

The Company soon introduced a metal holder marked "Coca-Cola" specially made to hold straight-sided glasses. This holder transformed an unmarked glass into a Coca-Cola glass. Examples of both the straight-sided glasses and the nickel silver holders have survived, although they are quite rare. Collectors should be aware that The Coca-Cola Company reproduced the metal holder in the 1970s.

FLARE GLASSES

In 1905, the Company introduced a new shape glass for Coca-Cola. It had a small diameter at the base, flaring out to a much larger diameter at the rim. Although today's collectors usually refer to these as "flare glasses", at the time it was introduced, this glass was called a "bell" glass for obvious reasons – when inverted, it has the same basic shape as a bell. This glass – the bell or flare glass – for the next two decades became a sight so familiar throughout the world that the very shape of the glass was instantly associated with Coca-Cola.

In 1923, the Company introduced a new glass with a turned edge at the rim. Called a "modified flare glass" by today's collectors, this glass was widely touted at Company functions as the perfect glass for Coca-Cola. By 1926, four million modified flare glasses had been sold for fountain use. The Coca-Cola glass underwent another significant change in 1929 when the turned edge at the top was made even more pronounced, giving the glass a distinct bulge about half an inch from the top. From an engineering standpoint, this pronounced bulge lowered the centre of gravity of the glass and made it harder to tip over. And even if it were knocked over, the point of impact was lower on the glass, thereby making it even more unlikely that the glass would chip at the top. The glass industry called this

ABOVE **Rice-paper fan, c. 1905, 25 × 38 cm (10 × 15 inches). By showing the current Coca-Cola glass on many different forms of advertising, the Company subliminally indoctrinated the public to think of Coca-Cola whenever they saw a flare glass.**

RIGHT **Cardboard cutout, 1935, 84 cm (33⅛ inches) high. Since 1929, the bell-shaped glass, seen here in a large Canadian cardboard cutout, has become the one most closely associated with Coca-Cola worldwide.**

RIGHT **Flare glass, c. 1910; large 3p (5¢) glass, 1912, and small 3p (5¢) glass, 1913, each approximately 10 cm (4 inches) high. Shown here are three examples of the flare glasses that were in common use in soda fountains from 1905 to the early 1920s.**

LEFT **Modified-flare glass, c. 1925, 9 cm (3¾ inches) high. Because the rim of a flare glass was so easily chipped when knocked over, Coca-Cola glasses were slightly modified in 1923 to alleviate this problem.**

ABOVE **Bell-shaped glass, 1936, 10 cm (4 inches) high. Every person at The Coca-Cola Fountain Sales Corporation's Fiftieth Anniversary Dinner was** presented with a personalized bell-shaped glass. Peter J Hunter, this glass's recipient, was a district manager for the corporation.

ABOVE **Straight-sided glass, 1958, 14 cm (5⅝ inches) high. Non-standard Coca-Cola glasses have been issued periodically to note special occasions. This** commemorative glass was produced to honour John M Jones on his thirty-fifth anniversary as President of the San Diego (California) Bottling Company.

a "cupped" glass, but today's collectors, somewhat confusingly, call it a "bell" glass.

Thus, by 1930 the evolution in the shape of the Coca-Cola glass had ended. The syrup line had disappeared because fountain dispensers now automatically dispensed the correct amount of Coca-Cola syrup. Only one significant change in glasses has taken place since that time. In the spring of 1955, The Coca-Cola Company broke with tradition and began test marketing 355 ml (twelve-ounce) glasses of Coca-Cola at soda fountains in New York and Los Angeles. This new glass was an instant success. The 355 ml (twelve-ounce) glass was followed in 1961 by a 474 ml (sixteen-ounce) "Jumbo" to accommodate a scoop of ice cream for the "Float with Coke" campaign.

Since the 1960s, fountain glasses for Coca-Cola have undergone countless major changes. Although bell-shaped

glasses are still available in a variety of sizes, other shapes, often with colourful printing portraying cartoon characters or traditional Coca-Cola artwork, are extensively used, especially as part of promotions at fast-food outlets also. The popularity of paper and plastic cups has also considerably changed the fountain glass picture.

As with any item issued year after year, there are distinct collectible differences within each category of Coca-Cola glasses. For example, glasses may have a single, double or broken syrup line; the word "Drink" may be missing or replaced by the word "Bottle" or "Enjoy"; the trademark notification may be different or missing; and the glass may be marked with a small or large "5¢". Non-English versions of Coca-Cola glasses are also highly collectible, as well as those created for Coca-Cola sponsored events such as the Olympics.

ABOVE **Fountain dispenser, c. 1930, 38 × 29 × 44 cm (15 × 11½ × 17½ inches). Post-mix counter dispensers, such as this one made by the Multiplex Faucet** Company of St Louis, Missouri, **automatically combined carbonated water with the correct amount of Coca-Cola syrup as the handle was turned.**

ABOVE **Paper cups, c. 1950, 1957, and 1961, each approximately 9 cm (3¾ inches) high. Coca-Cola cups were first introduced in 1941, but did not achieve** **widespread use until after World War II. The cups shown here were used with pre-mix machines which dispensed the finished product, already mixed at the bottling plant.**

BELOW **Box of straws, 1957, 22 cm (8⅝ inches) high. Although this box of 250 straws shows a paper cup, straws were also used with glasses and bottles.**

OTHER FOUNTAIN ITEMS

Fountain dispensing machines marked "Coca-Cola" and "Coke" from all periods are also popular collector's items today. However, few collectors have them in working order because the mechanisms needed to make them function properly are both bulky and hard to maintain.

Paper napkins, coasters and straws marked Coca-Cola – often used in conjunction with Coca-Cola glasses – are also collected. Amazingly, some pre-1900 tissue paper napkins imprinted with Coca-Cola slogans have survived. Coasters, usually round in shape, also feature a number of designs and messages. There are even straws marked "Coca-Cola". The variety, colourfulness and availability of such items enhance them as collectibles.

BOTTLES

HUTCHINSON BOTTLES

The earliest bottles used for Coca-Cola contained only the syrup, not the carbonated beverage we know today. John Pemberton, who invented Coca-Cola in 1886, used plain bottles with paper labels marked "Coca-Cola Syrup and Extract" to distribute the syrup to soda fountains. At fountains the syrup was mixed with plain water and served to customers. At some point, carbonated water was used instead of plain water, and the vitalized drink became a soda fountain success. Then in 1894 Joseph A Biedenharn of Vicksburg, Mississippi, put the carbonated beverage in bottles so that people could enjoy the soft drink away from soda fountains.

The first bottles to contain carbonated Coca-Cola were Biedenharn's soda water bottles marked "Biedenharn Candy Co., Vicksburg, Miss.", bottles that he had used previously for other beverages. They were not marked with the Coca-Cola trademark. These thick-walled, 178 ml (six-ounce) bottles used Hutchinson stoppers rather than the bottle caps with which we are familiar today. In 1897, the second bottler to put carbonated Coca-Cola in bottles was the Valdosta (Georgia) Bottling Works owned by R H Holmes and E R Barber. Their Hutchinson-stopper bottles were marked "Valdosta Electric Bottling Works, Valdosta, Ga.", and like the Biedenharn bottles were not marked "Coca-Cola".

In 1899, Benjamin F Thomas and Joseph B Whitehead, two lawyers from Chattanooga, Tennessee, were convinced that bottling Coca-Cola was a good business idea. They arranged to meet Asa Candler, president of The Coca-Cola Company. After being assured that they would take full responsibility for bottling operations, Candler gave Thomas and Whitehead exclusive rights to bottle Coca-Cola in the entire United States except for the territories covered by pre-existing contracts in the New England

LEFT **Hutchinson-stopper bottle, c. 1902, 17 cm (6¾ inches) high. Unlike many early bottles that are discoloured and worn, this bottle from Birmingham, Alabama, complete with the Hutchinson stopper, is a particularly fine example of the first bottles used for Coca-Cola.**

To open such a bottle, one had to push down on the wire loop, an action that produced a loud popping sound – the origin of the term "soda pop".

states, Mississippi and Texas. The first bottles marked "Coca-Cola" to be used in this new business enterprise were Hutchinson-stopper bottles. The use of Hutchinson bottles for Coca-Cola was short-lived since within two years the more dependable and cheaper crown-top bottles became the industry standard.

CROWN-TOP BOTTLES

Bottlers soon switched over to the new crown-top bottles. Bottles were hand-blown, glass was mixed in relatively small batches, and bottle sizes were not standardized. The result for today's collectors is a seemingly endless variety of bottles in different shapes, colours and sizes, with previously unknown bottles still surfacing today. However, collectors generally separate early bottles into two main categories: amber bottles, ranging in colour from dark brown to the colour of honey; and more transparent bottles including green, blue, aqua and colourless.

These early crown-top bottles were identified as containing Coca-Cola by at least one of the following three devices: (1) the trademark "Coca-Cola" was blown into the glass; (2) the bottle cap was marked with the trademark; and (3) a diamond-shaped paper label printed with the trademark was glued to the side of the bottle. At least nine different versions of authentic paper labels have survived, but they have also been heavily reproduced so that today's collectors often need to consult experts to tell the difference. Buyers should beware of paying premium prices for old bottles to which reproduction labels have

ABOVE **Bottles with paper labels, c. 1910, clear, 20 cm (7¾ inches) high, and amber, 19 cm (7½ inches) high. Shown here are typical examples of the two colours of bottles used from 1905 to about 1920. Some bottlers thought darker bottles preserved the flavour of Coca-Cola better than lighter bottles.**

RIGHT **Cardboard cutout, 1937, 112 cm (44⅛ inches) high. Since the hobbleskirt bottle was introduced in 1916, it has been prominently featured in the advertising for Coca-Cola.**

been attached. Bottles first appeared on standard artwork advertising Coca-Cola in 1903 and were clear straight-sided bottles with diamond-shaped paper labels. Thereafter, the Company often produced two versions of their annual calendars and other advertising items: one for fountain sales and a nearly identical version to which a straight-sided bottle with a diamond-shaped paper label had been added.

The Coca-Cola Company finally addressed the need for a standardized bottle for Coca-Cola, mainly to fight the growing problem of imitators. B F Thomas put it this way: "We need a bottle which a person can recognize as a Coca-Cola bottle when he feels it in the dark". Bottle manufacturers were invited to submit designs for consideration, and a seven-man committee at the annual 1916 Coca-Cola Bottlers Convention made the final decision. The winning design derived its inspiration from a line drawing of a cocoa pod (which had been mistaken for a coca bean), and was patented 16 November, 1915. The glass colour selected was a light shade of green known as "German green" at the time, but now called "Georgia green" in honour of the home state of Coca-Cola. The prototype bottle, which had an exaggerated bulge around the middle, was then modified to fit automatic bottling equipment. Only two known examples of the original prototype bottle exist, although the bottle was reproduced in 1971 and again in 1986 by the Company.

BELOW **Bottles, 1986, each 19 cm (7½ inches) high. As the world's most recognized container, the hobbleskirt bottle has been produced for international use.** Shown here from left to right are bottles from China, Bulgaria, Morocco, Japan, United States, Thailand, Korea, Israel and Ethiopia.

ABOVE **Bottle, 1967, 20 cm (7¾ inches) high. When Coca-Cola bottlers began marketing "no-deposit" bottles – ones that were not meant to be returned to the** bottler – in the late 1960s, they again turned to straight-sided bottles with paper labels.

By 1920, the new standardized bottle – called a hobbleskirt bottle because its shape resembled a dress fashion of the day – was in widespread use throughout the United States. The 16 November, 1915, patent date was blown into the glass just below the Coca-Cola trademark. After renewing the bottle patent in 1923 and registering the shape of the bottle as a design patent in 1937, the Company finally registered the classic hobbleskirt bottle as a trademark on 12 April, 1960. Some collectors specialize in these hobbleskirt bottles and have accumulated bottles from every state and of every possible variation. The value of these bottles depends largely upon rarity and condition.

CANS, CASES, CARTONS AND CARRIERS

Beginning in the mid-1950s, closed containers other than hobbleskirt bottles were introduced. Coca-Cola was first packaged in flat-top cans in 1955, but on a limited basis for overseas American military personnel. The late 1960s and early 1970s saw the first widespread use of non-returnable bottles, first made of glass and later plastic. The proliferation of containers for Coca-Cola in glass, metal and plastic continues to this day. Consequently, collectors who specialize in bottles or cans face a daunting task indeed to acquire all the containers ever used for Coca-Cola.

Cases, cartons and carriers are also associated with collecting bottles. At first, bottles of Coca-Cola were transported in traditional 24-bottle wooden cases stenciled with the trademark "Coca-Cola". These cases were used to take the bottles from the bottling plants to the shops, although some bottlers sold 24-bottle cases directly to consumers. Since 24 bottles were too many for the average consumer at one time, the Company introduced the six-bottle cardboard carton in the mid-1920s. While the cardboard carrier continues to this day, the intervening years witnessed a parade of carriers made of wood, metal and plastic. Because of a lack of standardization for cases, cartons and carriers, there are countless examples for today's collectors.

LEFT **Cardboard bottle toppers, 1939, each 33 cm (13 inches) high. The hobbleskirt bottle itself was often incorporated into displays, as shown by this pair of German "bottle toppers".**

RIGHT **Bottles, 1920–1950, each 20 cm (7¾ inches) high. In addition to Coca-Cola, most bottlers also sold other flavours such as orange, grape, cherry, lime and root beer. The bottles used for these drinks were called "flavour bottles" and usually carried the bottler's name with Coca-Cola in block letters, instead of script.**

CANS

ABOVE **Can, 1956, 13 cm (4⅞ inches) high. The first flat-topped cans for Coca-Cola were prepared by the Hayward, California, bottler in 1955 for shipment to American servicemen in the Pacific and by the New Bedford, Massachusetts, bottler in 1956 for shipment to Europe. These all-steel cans were made available throughout the United States beginning in 1959.**

ABOVE **Can, 1980, 13 cm (4⅞ inches) high. Although Coca-Cola was not sold in the Soviet Union in 1980, the Company arranged to supply the Olympic Village with Coca-Cola for the Moscow Olympics. The cans, made in Baltimore, Maryland, were never shipped because of President Carter's decision to withdraw the United States team from competition.**

LEFT **Can, 1994, 13 cm (4⅞ inches) high. Since the late 1960s, most Coca-Cola cans have been made from aluminium and steel. Ironically, one of the most recent versions features the classic hobbleskirt bottle in its design.**

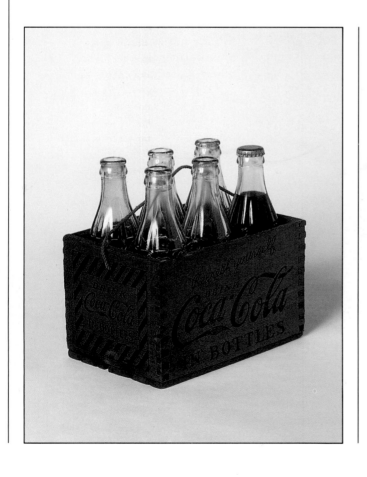

LEFT **Wooden carrier, c. 1926, 20 × 14 × 13 cm (8⅛ × 5½ × 5 inches). With dove-tailed corners and rope handle, this finely crafted carrier was one of the earliest forerunners of the now-familiar six-pack carton.**

ABOVE **12-bottle box, 1932, 36 × 21 × 14 cm (14 × 8¼ × 5½ inches). Not content to have customers carry bottles of Coca-Cola home six at a time, the Los Angeles bottler pioneered the 12-bottle box.**

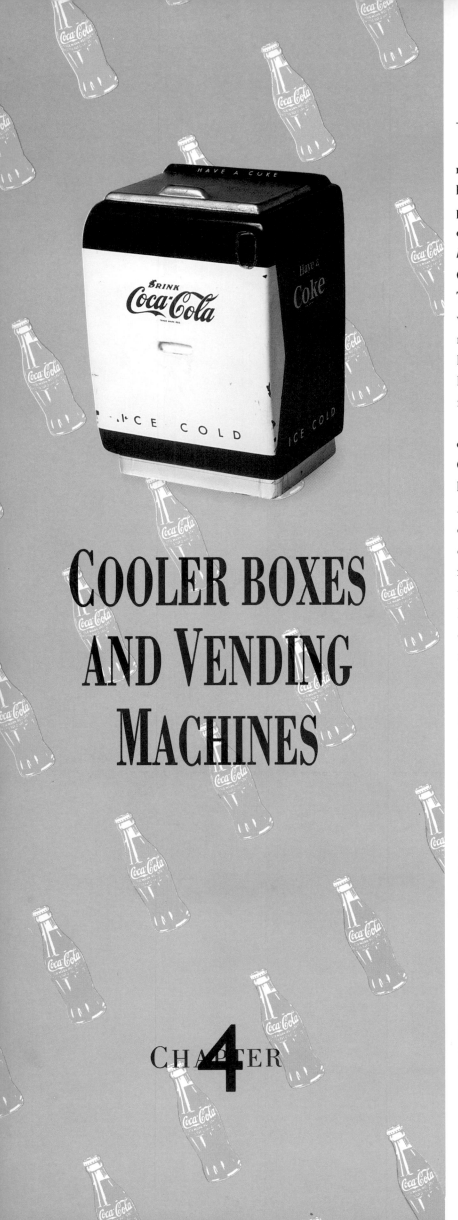

COOLER BOXES AND VENDING MACHINES

When the sale of Coca-Cola in bottles first began around the turn of the century, it was the responsibility of the retailer (often a grocer) to see that the bottles were kept chilled. Most accomplished this by placing the bottles in their shop's ice-boxes, along with the eggs, butter, cheese, meat, etc. Since these other products *had* to be kept cold to avoid spoilage, and bottles of Coca-Cola did not, keeping the bottles cold was a low priority. The average grocer kept only a few bottles on ice; and when they were sold, new ones weren't always replaced right away. Consequently, when a customer bought a bottle of Coca-Cola, it wasn't always as cold as it should have been since the proper coldness enhances both the flavour of Coca-Cola and the effects of carbonation.

It didn't take long for some enterprising bottler to figure out that if he supplied the grocer with a cooler box just for Coca-Cola, then an ample supply of properly chilled bottles would always be available for thirsty customers. Additionally, there was the added advertising that such a cooler box would provide – no small matter in a highly competitive field. The first cooler boxes made especially for bottled Coca-Cola were believed to have been barrels that had been cut in half to form tubs in which ice and bottles could be kept. Advertising was added by stenciled or metal signs. Placed in a conspicuous location, often right inside the front door, this combination of ice and bottles practically begged a customer to have an ice-cold bottle of Coca-Cola, especially on a hot day. Such a half-barrel tub is an example of a "wet cooler box", where melting ice rather than electricity provides the cooling.

With the increasing popularity of bottled Coca-Cola, numerous bottlers devised more successful wet cooler boxes which were nothing more than wooden boxes on legs. A sliding or hinged lid along with a metal lining completed the design. More often than not, the outer wooden case was painted with what later became called "Coca-Cola yellow", with stenciled advertising in "Coca-Cola red". These display boxes were used at a variety of

LEFT **Miniature cooler box, 1956, 15 × 13 × 23cm (6 × 5 × 8⅞ inches). Handmade from a single block of wood, this miniature is a faithful reproduction of the white-faced cooler box, used in the late 1950s.**

ABOVE **Bottle in dry server, c. 1931, 10 × 17 cm (3⅞ × 6¾ inches). Because early Coca-Cola coolers chilled the bottles by immersing them in an ice-water bath, a paper sleeve wrapped around the bottle prevented the excess moisture from dripping on the customer.**

locations in addition to grocery stores. The ready availability of vending machines today in shops, at places of employment, on sidewalks, and at special events, such as ball games, fairs and picnics, make it difficult to imagine that such an idea was once new.

The next advance in cooler box manufacture in the mid-1920s replaced the wooden exterior with one made of sheet metal. The interior still consisted of a tub filled with ice water to cool the bottles. Additional design features included mechanisms that required customers to insert a warm bottle of soda in order to remove a cold bottle and coin-operated mechanisms that permitted the customer to get only one bottle of soda for a nickel. Both innovations made the operation of these cooler boxes more automatic and less bother to the shop owner.

As part of their standardization efforts in 1928, The Coca-Cola Company decided that uniformity was essential if Coca-Cola were to be recognized by the public as the same quality drink throughout the world. After comparing all the popular cooler boxes in use at the time, a prototype was developed by the Company. The Glascock Brothers Manufacturing Company of Muncie, Indiana, was chosen to make the new cooler box, and it was introduced at the 1929 annual convention of Coca-Cola bottlers. Glascock cooler boxes were sold, rather than given, to retailers.

LEFT **Salesman's sample cooler box, 1929, 27 × 20 × 34 cm (10½ × 7¾ × 13⅜ inches). Because Coca-Cola cooler boxes were sold, not given, to retailers, Coca-Cola salesmen were furnished with this miniature version of the Glascock cooler box so that they could demonstrate its features without having to transport the full-sized model along with them.**

ABOVE **Salesman's sample cooler box, 1939, 30 × 18 × 25 cm (12⅛ × 7¼ × 10⅛ inches). Although the Coca-Cola cooler box was redesigned in 1934, it** **was not until 1939 that a salesman's sample was produced as part of the "Business Builders" cooler box sales contest in that year.**

Because of the Glascock cooler box's superior insulation, the savings on the cost of ice enabled the retailer to recoup the cost of the cooler box in less than a year. Unlike many of its predecessors, many examples of the Glascock cooler box, even ones used in non-English speaking countries, have survived for today's collectors.

Although immensely popular, the Glascock cooler box was replaced in 1934 by a new cooler box with rounded corners. Westinghouse was the exclusive manufacturer the first year, and the Cavalier Corporation began making them as well the following year. Prior to World War II, nearly all the cooler boxes used for Coca-Cola were ice cooled. Although electric cooler boxes had been available from Glascock as early as 1930, few were sold because they cost approximately ten times as much as wet cooler boxes. In 1945, the Company introduced a new streamlined cooler box conceived by internationally renowned industrial designer Raymond Loewy. In addition to other improvements, Loewy's award-winning design featured a completely enclosed base concealing the electric refrigeration unit which by now had become standard. This cooler box was the model for the late 1940s cooler-box-shaped radio and music boxes.

ABOVE **Cooler box savings bank, c. 1940, 8 × 11 × 3 cm (3⅛ × 4¼ × 1 inches). Produced by Zell Products Company of New York, this bank was given to retailers so that they could save the £12.90 (20 dollars) needed to buy their own cooler boxes.**

RIGHT **Cardboard cutout, 1937, 90 cm (35½ inches) high. The red cooler box, as it was commonly called, was incorporated into Coca-Cola advertising so that when thirsty customers entered a shop, they would know what to look for.**

The late 1940s and early 1950s marked the change from horizontal cooler boxes to vertical vending machines. Now a machine did more than just cool the bottles: it handled the entire financial transaction including making change. Taken as a group, the vending machines produced after 1950 form a bewildering array of shapes, uses and manufacturers. Vending machines were even used to dispense paper cups with Coca-Cola and cracked ice. Today most machines dispense cans of Coca-Cola. Many collectors have at least one working cooler box or vending machine stocked with Coca-Cola for entertaining guests. While few collectors have the space to accumulate very many cooler boxes and vending machines, there are numerous associated collectibles that are considerably less bulky. Sales items such as miniature salesman samples, brochures, booklets and assorted novelties are highly prized.

BELOW **Vending machine, 1951, 63 × 62 × 164 cm (24¾ × 24½ × 64½ inches). Upright vending machines for Coca-Cola were introduced shortly before World War II. This post-war model was called a "C–51" because it was made by the Cavalier Corporation and vended fifty-one bottles.**

ABOVE **Paper folder, 1941, 23 × 31 cm (9¼ × 12¼ inches). This folder, die-cut in the shape of the 1941 Coca-Cola cooler box, was** used to advertise the coin-controlled mechanism made by the Vendo Company of Kansas City, Missouri.

PICNIC COOLER BOXES

ABOVE **Paper flyer, c. 1950, 22 × 18 cm (8½ × 7¼ inches). As Americans became more mobile after World War II, well-insulated metal picnic cooler boxes became standard household items. This flyer shows a model that was designed to hold "twelve bottles of Coca-Cola plus a generous amount of cracked ice".**

LEFT **Vinyl-covered picnic cooler box, 1964, 22 × 15 × 26 cm (8½ × 5⅞ × 10¼ inches). As part of a promotion for the 1964–65 New York World's Fair, the Company offered consumers this six-bottle cooler box.**

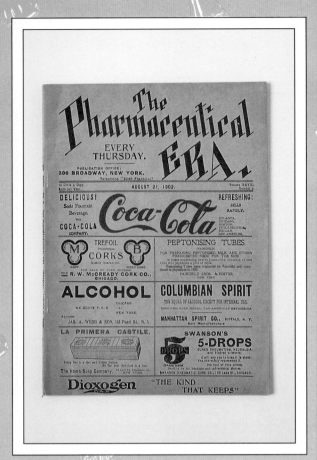

PERIODICAL ADVERTISING

Advertisements in newspapers and magazines constituted the earliest form of mass media used to advertise Coca-Cola. Because advertising and articles in periodicals have been produced regularly from Coca-Cola's beginnings, they are a rich source not only of collectibles, but also of information about Coca-Cola. Collectors are only beginning to realize the value of collecting such advertising. Because of the reasonable price of periodical advertising, even novice collectors are able to quickly and easily accumulate an impressive collection of original newspaper and magazine advertisements, commonly called "ads". Collectors must be cautious, however. With the advent of colour copiers, unscrupulous individuals can, and have, produced photocopies that are difficult to discern from originals.

Coca-Cola was first advertised in *The Daily Journal* newspaper in Atlanta on 29 May, 1886. The now familiar script Coca-Cola trademark had not yet been created, and "Coca-Cola" appeared in plain block letters. The advertisement read as follows: "Coca-Cola, Delicious, Refreshing, Exhilarating, Invigorating, The New and Popular Soda Fountain Drink, containing the properties of the wonderful Coca plant and the famous Cola nuts. For sale by Willis Venable and Nunnally & Rawson". In more than a dozen ads in 1886, Coca-Cola appeared in block letters, not script. The first known use of script Coca-Cola appeared in *The Daily Journal* on 16 June, 1887. It read simply, "Coca-Cola, Delicious, Refreshing, Exhilarating, Invigorating", and appeared unchanged throughout most of the rest of the summer of 1887. It is interesting to note that the phrase "Coca-Cola, Delicious, Refreshing" appeared in the first known advertisement for Coca-Cola and over the years has continued to be the most used phrase in its advertising.

Trade publications were the next type of periodical in which Coca-Cola was advertised. Beginning in the 1890s, Coca-Cola was heavily promoted in trade publications published for owners and employees of drug stores and soda fountains. These advertisements often explained how much profit could be made by selling Coca-Cola. In addition, these publications occasionally carried articles about Coca-Cola itself. Around the turn of the century,

LEFT **Magazine advertisement, 1902, 28 × 20 cm (11 × 8⅛ inches). Because drug stores and chemists at the turn of the** century typically had soda fountain counters, the Company advertised in trade publications such as *The Pharmaceutical Era.*

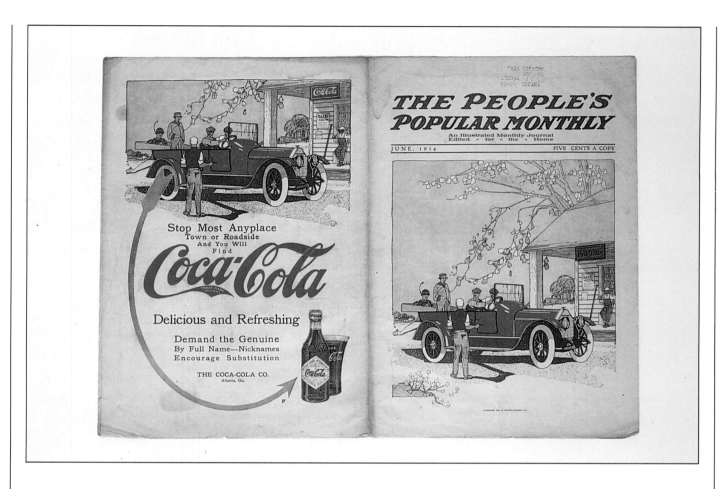

ABOVE **Magazine advertisement, 1914, 55 × 39 cm (21½ × 15⅜ inches). In a series of magazine "ads" in the 1910s, the back-cover advertisement for Coca-Cola incorporated the same artwork that was shown on the magazine's front cover.**

trade publications for the advertising business began to appear. Articles detailing advertising campaigns or gimmicks used by The Coca-Cola Company were frequently included. In order to attract more business, sign and novelty manufacturers sometimes placed full-colour advertisements showcasing, as examples of their manufacturing capabilities, the Coca-Cola items they had produced.

For the first time in 1904, The Coca-Cola Company placed advertisements in national consumer magazines. The same black-and-white ad was placed in six nationally distributed magazines. This advertisement featured Hilda Clark, the Coca-Cola calendar girl from 1903, and read, "Drink Coca-Cola at Soda Fountains and Carbonated in Bottles 5¢". In the years 1905 through 1907, national magazine advertising for Coca-Cola blossomed, featuring a variety of original artworks, many in full colour. Some of the advertisements produced during this time rank as the most collectible Coca-Cola advertising ever.

The advertising artwork used in national magazines changed every year. This annual change makes magazine advertisements one of the most fascinating areas of Coca-Cola collecting, since virtually every phase of American life was depicted at one time or another. During this same

RIGHT **Magazine advertisement, 1933, 34 × 28 cm (13½ × 10½ inches). The entire cast of the motion picture *Dinner at Eight* (including Jean Harlow and Lionel Barrymore) was featured in this 30 September, 1933, advertisement in *Saturday Evening Post*.**

period, newspaper advertising also flourished. Some newspaper ads used the same artwork as magazines, while others advertised local events along with the name, location and telephone number of the local bottler. While most newspaper advertisements are black and white covering only a portion of a page, there are also full-page examples in colour.

In addition to advertising in magazines and newspapers, The Coca-Cola Company and local bottlers began to advertise aggressively in local publications such as telephone and city directories, high school and college annuals, church bulletins and programmes for theatres, circuses and athletic events. Most of these employed artwork or graphics not used elsewhere and hence form an interesting sidelight to the regular advertising for Coca-Cola. The Coca-Cola Company also published periodicals and one-time publications for the general public. Household entertaining and decorating hints were featured in such publications as the *When You Entertain* book, the *Flower Arranging* books and the *Pause for Living* booklets.

Starting in 1896, another category of monthly periodical, this time for people in the Coca-Cola business, began with the introduction of *The Coca-Cola News* in Seth W Fowle's New England territory. The masthead of that publication declared that it "sheds light on subjects peculiar to the soda fountain". *The Coca-Cola Bottler* magazine began in 1909 for employees of the local bottlers. In 1921, *The Friendly Hand* newsletter was started for employees of The Coca-Cola Company. This latter publication was superseded in 1924 by *The Red Barrel* magazine, which was distributed to a broader audience, including soda fountain operators and bottler employees. In 1948, *Coca-Cola Overseas* debuted and contained stories, as the name suggests, about Coca-Cola sales operations outside the United States. In 1953, *The Red Barrel* ceased publication with the introduction of the *Refresher* magazine. Generally referred to as "in-house" magazines, these publications have pictures of the then-current advertising available, articles about improving sales of Coca-Cola, stories about Coca-Cola employees and general company news.

ABOVE **Magazine advertisement, 1914, 25 × 39 cm (9¾ × 15½ inches).** Advertising for Coca-Cola, the great American drink, often teamed Coca-Cola with baseball, the great American pastime.

ABOVE **Baseball program, 1930, 18 × 28 cm (7 × 10⅞ inches).** In keeping with its long-standing association with baseball, Coca-Cola was frequently advertised in baseball programs such as this one from Baltimore, Maryland.

BELOW **Magazine advertisement, 1922, 25 × 35 cm (10 × 13¾ inches).** Prior to World War I, soft drinks were thought of and advertised as being primarily summertime drinks. In the 1920s, the Company began vigorously promoting Coca-Cola as the drink that "knows no season".

BELOW **Magazine advertisement, 1957, 27 × 34 cm (10¾ × 13½ inches).** Shown here is one of a short-lived series of advertisements with stylized artwork showing people enjoying Coca-Cola at various locations throughout the world.

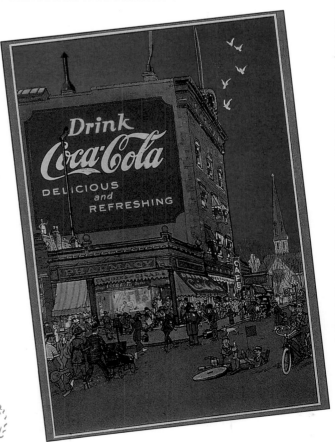

ABOVE **Magazine advertisement, 1947, 25 × 34 cm (10 × 13½ inches). Post-war teenage American life was idealized in Coca-Cola ads such as this soda fountain scene from the 10 February, 1947, issue of** *Life*.

BELOW **Magazine advertisement, 1907, 27 × 38 cm (10⅜ × 14⅞ inches). In keeping with the slogan that identified Coca-Cola as "The Great National Drink", it was appropriate that Uncle Sam and the US Capitol building would be featured in magazine advertising.**

ABOVE **Newspaper advertisement, 1908, 39 × 53 cm (15½ × 21 inches). Because of the cost involved, it was very unusual for Coca-Cola to be advertised in full-page colour newspaper advertisements such as this example from the** *Sunday American-Examiner*.

BELOW **Magazine advertisement, 1920, 20 × 30 cm (8 × 11¾ inches). One of the most beloved magazine advertising campaigns for Coca-Cola in the 1920s used cartoon drawings to portray small-town life such as that shown in this corner chemist scene.**

CALENDARS

The earliest known Coca-Cola calendar dates from 1891, and the Company has issued annual calendars from that point on. Starting in the mid-1890s, the artwork used on the Coca-Cola calendar was also used on other advertising issued the same year. What was employed at this early date is an advanced and sophisticated advertising concept known today as a unified campaign, where the same image is used on all kinds of advertising for a particular period of time. Fortunately for collectors, The Coca-Cola Company used this advertising strategy well into the 1950s. Since many advertising items do not have a date printed on them, this practice is especially helpful for dating items that have the same artwork as that year's calendar.

It is now generally agreed among collectors that the date associated with a collectible is its year of first use as established by the artwork on the annual Coca-Cola calendar, even though the item itself may carry an earlier copyright date. For example, because the 1913 Coca-Cola calendar was prepared for distribution in late 1912, its artwork was copyrighted in 1912. The 1912 copyright date is printed in the calendar's lower left corner, while the 1913 date appears only on the calendar pages. In the absence of these pages, one might erroneously mistake the 1912 copyright date to be the year of use. Trays showing the same artwork were marked with the 1912 copyright date only. However, these trays were not used until 1913 and are therefore correctly called "1913 trays" today.

In 1904, the Company and parent bottlers began issuing different calendars each year, one for fountain sales and the other for the sale of Coca-Cola in bottles. In most instances, the very same artwork was used, but one version showed a glass of Coca-Cola, while the other showed a bottle. In some years, entirely different artwork was used for the two versions. The last calendars handled in this way were the 1927 ones, although the practice of having bottle versus glass variations on other items continued into the 1940s.

LEFT **Calendar, 1911, 27 × 46 cm (10¾ × 18 inches). With artwork copyrighted in 1909, this is one of several Coca-Cola calendars created by the American illustrator Hamilton King, whose signature appears on the calendar.**

LEFT **Calendar, 1908, 18 × 36 cm (7 × 14⅛ inches). The note on the table reads "Good to the Last Drop", a slogan that was later adopted and trademarked by Maxwell House Coffee, one of the leading American coffees sold.**

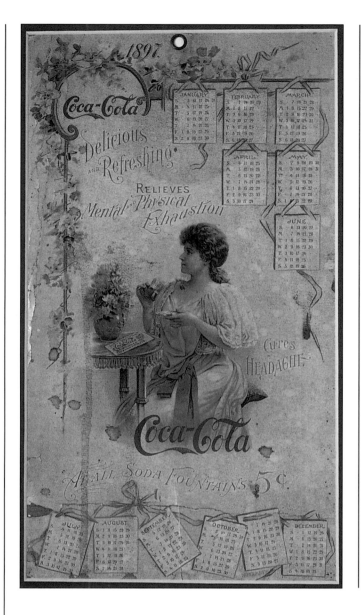

ABOVE **Calendar, 1897, 19 × 33 cm (7½ × 13 inches). The artwork on this calendar has been dubbed the "Victorian Girl". Interestingly, examples of the free-drink Coca-Cola coupon seen on the table in the artwork have survived.**

In addition to Company-issued calendars, some local Coca-Cola bottlers produced their own calendars as early as the 1930s. These calendars featured stock artwork (not prepared especially for Coca-Cola) showing such things as landscapes, wildlife and Boy Scouts. Since these calendars were distributed to businesses and homes within the local bottler's territory, they were imprinted with the bottler's name, address and telephone number.

Not only did the Company produce calendars for use in the United States, but for foreign markets as well. Examples from the 1930s and 1940s generally used the indigenous languages, but carried the same artwork as used on American advertising items. Slight modifications were sometimes made to the artwork, such as changing blond hair to brunette for Latin American countries. Examples from the 1950s typically portray the language, people and culture of the country where the calendar was distributed.

ABOVE **Calendar, 1904, 21 × 39 cm (8¼ × 15¼ inches). Breaking an unwritten rule of not advertising using children, this calendar portraying a child holding a bottle of Coca-Cola is unusual for its day.**

RIGHT **Calendar, 1918, 33 × 79 cm (13 × 31⅛ inches). Because of sugar shortages during World War I which reduced production, The Coca-Cola Company advertised very little during 1918. Although Coca-Cola calendars before and after this one were produced in two versions, bottle and glass, only this version was produced in 1918.**

BELOW **Calendar, 1916, 20 × 38 cm (8 × 15 inches). Appearing as an insert in the Sunday edition of the *New York World* newspaper, this summer calendar shows only three months. The model is actress Pearl White, famous for her role in the silent-movie serial *The Perils of Pauline*.**

LEFT **Calendar, 1936, 30 × 63 cm (12 × 24¾ inches). Imprinted with the logo for the fiftieth anniversary of Coca-Cola, this calendar, created by illustrator N C Wyeth, carries artwork typical of the Coca-Cola calendars during the 1930s.**

BELOW **Distributor calendar, 1928, 20 × 35 cm (7¾ × 13¾ inches). Bearing the name of a specific retailer, this distributor calendar was a small-sized version of the regular Coca-Cola calendar used for 1928.**

ABOVE **Calendar, 1954, 33 × 48 cm (13 × 19⅛ inches). Showing a series of Egyptian movie actresses, this four-page calendar was printed in a combination of both Arabic and French for distribution in the Middle East.**

The annual calendars up to 1940 in the United States consisted of a single artwork which was visible for the entire year of use. After that, calendars used at least six pages, each with a different artwork and a calendar for two consecutive months. Hence, unlike the earlier calendars, the picture changed every two months.

Most of these calendars were intended to be displayed in places of business where Coca-Cola was sold. In 1954, The Coca-Cola Company introduced the "home calendar", a small calendar sent directly to customers' homes. Also called reference calendars, they carried useful bits of information such as the dates of holidays, state flowers and birds, signs of the zodiac, birthstones for each month, first-aid hints, entertaining tips and equivalents for kitchen measurements.

Starting in the 1960s, smaller business calendars called "calendar displays" were distributed. They consisted of a metal back plate, which carried the advertising for Coca-Cola, and two screw-in posts designed to hold calendar sheets for every day of the year. Once installed, all that needed to be replaced from year to year were the calendar pads. High-quality desk calendars with subtle Coca-Cola advertising were also given to high-volume customers and outstanding employees.

ABOVE **Calendar, 1943, 33 × 51 cm (13 × 20 inches). In keeping with the spirit of the time, this six-page calendar shows women in war-related roles. Shown here on the January/February page is a US Army Nurse.**

ABOVE **Calendar display, 1961, 24 × 32 cm (9⅜ × 12¾ inches).** Although the so-called "arciform" logo at the top of this item was not used on any new Coca-Cola advertising after 1963, the durability of a metal calendar display probably would have ensured its use well after that date.

BELOW **Desk calendar, 1952, 16 cm (6¼ inches) wide.** Changing the plastic date cards provided with this high-quality bronze desk calendar meant it could be used for any month and year.

ABOVE **Home calendar, 1955, 18 × 15 cm (7 × 6 inches).** Because they were generally distributed by bottlers as Christmas gifts, "home calendars" often showed Santa Claus on the cover page.

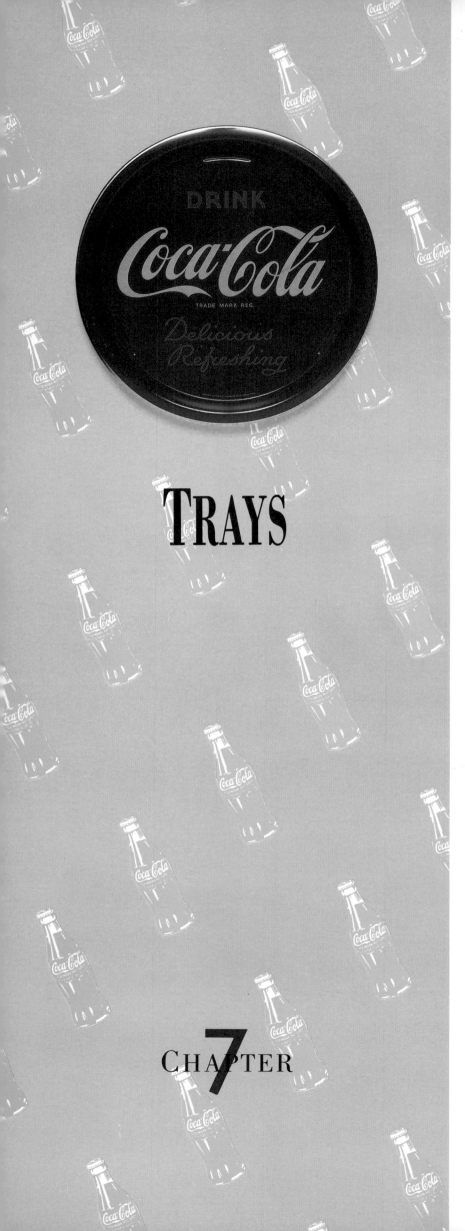

TRAYS

Perhaps no other form of the vast array of items that have been used to advertise Coca-Cola over the years is as closely associated with the product as the "Coca-Cola tray". Beginning in the 1890s and continuing to this day, a series of metal trays has carried forth the "Drink Coca-Cola" message. The enduring qualities of metal, combined with the relatively large number that were produced, have guaranteed the survival of many trays for today's collectors.

Trays used to advertise Coca-Cola can be divided into three general categories depending on their intended use: serving trays, change trays and TV trays. A serving tray, as the name suggests, was meant for serving things, presumably glasses or bottles of Coca-Cola. Although they were frequently used as coasters and ashtrays, change trays were supposed to be used to return change to customers after they had paid their bills in soda fountains and restaurants. Since many a customer left a gratuity for the waiter or waitress on these very same trays, they are often called tip trays as well. Like their namesake, TV trays are a product of much more recent times. These trays were capable of carrying an entire meal from the kitchen to the living room, so that a person could sit in front of the television set and eat dinner at the same time.

The advertising novelty business, which included the manufacture of trays, is said to have started in Coshocton, Ohio. J F Meek, the publisher of a Coshocton weekly newspaper, was one of the pioneers in this business. In 1887 (one year after the beginning of Coca-Cola), Meek established a separate company, called the Tuscarora Advertising Company, to handle his growing advertising novelty business. His success was duly noted, and H D Beach, another Coshocton publisher, started his own novelty business in 1888 under the name of the Standard Advertising Company. Having common interests, it came as no surprise that in 1900 the two businessmen merged their respective businesses into one company calling it the Meek and Beach Company. Beach soon sold his interest to Meek and established the H D Beach Company. Meek soon shortened the name of the Meek and Beach Company

LEFT **Metal tray, c. 1950, 34 cm (12¾-inch) diameter. Made in London, this British tray might have been used to serve drinks at pubs and restaurants.**

CHAPTER 7

ABOVE **Metal tray, 1963, 47 × 34 cm (18⅝ × 13¼ inches). As seen on this Mexican TV tray, appetizing food and frosty bottles of Coca-Cola were the usual subject of these oversized trays.**

LEFT **Metal tray, 1903, 25-cm (9¾-inch) diameter. The "Bottle Tray" is one of the earliest advertising items to depict the then new straight-sided, paper-label bottle for Coca-Cola.**

ABOVE **Metal trays, 1910, 26 × 34 cm (10½ × 13¼ inches) and 11 × 15 cm (4⅜ × 6⅛ inches). Shown here side by side are the 1910 "Hamilton King Girl" rectangular serving tray and the companion oval change tray.**

to the Meek Company, and in 1909, changed it once more, this time to American Art Works. It was under that name that the company produced most of the trays for Coca-Cola from 1910 through the 1940s. As a consequence of all this tray-making activity in Coshocton, the flea markets, antique shops and estate sales in and around Coshocton still yield a large number of the older Coca-Cola trays for today's collectors.

A list of the Coshocton firms and the Coca-Cola trays they made follows: Standard Advertising Company, the 1900 Coca-Cola trays; The Meek and Beach Company, some of the 1901 Coca-Cola trays; The Meek Company, the rest of the 1901 Coca-Cola trays, as well as the 1905 Coca-Cola trays; The H D Beach Company, the 1909 and 1922 Coca-Cola trays; and American Art Works, the 1910 trays and the majority of the trays from 1923 to 1942

LEFT **Metal tray, 1909, 27 × 33 cm (10¾ × 13 inches). Called the "Exposition Girl" artwork, the scene in the background on this tray is typical of world's fairs of the Victorian era.**

RIGHT **Metal tray, 1922, 27 × 34 cm (10½ × 13¼ inches). Because the 1922 calendar bearing the same artwork reveals that the woman is actually at a baseball game, this tray is commonly called the "Baseball Girl" tray.**

inclusive. In addition to Coshocton-based companies, the following manufacturers also made Coca-Cola trays: Sentenne & Green (New York), the 1899 trays; Charles W Shonk Company (Chicago), the 1903 and 1907 trays; the NY Metal Ceiling Company (New York), the 1906 trays; Stelad Signs-Passaic Metal Ware Company (New Jersey), the 1913, 1914 and 1916 trays; and Tindeco (Baltimore), some of the 1927 and 1929 trays.

The earliest known tray featuring Coca-Cola dates from 1897. There is an interesting progression in the shape of American Coca-Cola trays, starting with all round trays before 1903, followed by a mixture of round, oval and rectangular trays through 1920, and concluding with all rectangular trays from 1921 on. The series ended with the production of the so-called Pansy trays in the 1960s. After that time, The Coca-Cola Company and others began issuing reproduction trays in many shapes. While the earlier trays were intended as useful items for Coca-Cola

BELOW **Metal tray, 1934, 33 × 27 cm (13¼ × 10½ inches). Former Olympic swimming champion Johnny Weissmuller and actress Maureen O'Sullivan, stars of a series of "Tarzan" movies produced by Metro-Goldwyn-Mayer, are shown on this tray.**

ABOVE **Metal tray, c. 1908, 31 cm (12¼-inch) diameter. Designed for the bar and tavern trade, this "Topless Tray" shows a model nude to the waist holding a** **bottle of Coca-Cola. It was produced not by The Coca-Cola Company in Atlanta, but rather by the Western Coca-Cola Bottling Company in Chicago.**

vendors, these reproduction trays were meant to appeal to a nostalgia-crazed American public. Reproduction trays are still being made today at an ever-increasing rate.

Exactly how many of the early trays were produced is not known since existing records are sketchy at best. It is known however that before the turn of the century, a tray manufacturer would make as few as fifty trays for a client. In view of the size of The Coca-Cola Company's advertising budget at the time, it is safe to assume that a considerably larger number of trays was produced for the Company's use. Records do tell us that by 1913, two million trays, all destined for fountain use, were being distributed annually. Prior to the late 1920s, most trays showed a glass rather than a bottle. As the sales of bottled Coca-Cola began to approach and eventually overtake fountain sales in 1928, the number of trays intended for fountain use declined as the number of trays for bottler use increased. After 1930, all standard Coca-Cola trays showed a bottle.

Since the Company ordered trays in such large quantities, the cost of an individual tray was kept to a minimum. Turn-of-the-century trays cost approximately 2p (3¢) each, while those throughout the 1920s and 1930s cost between 8p (12¢) and 10p (15¢) each. Between World War II and the 1960s, the price ranged from 16p (24¢) to 30p (45¢) each. While these prices may seem ridiculously low by today's collecting standards, one must remember that these trays were being used to advertise a product that cost only 3p (5¢) per serving as recently as the early 1950s.

Although a few examples of Coca-Cola trays were produced for foreign markets as early as the 1920s, most foreign Coca-Cola trays date from after World War II. In particular, numerous trays were produced for use in both Mexico and Canada. As the interest in collecting Coca-Cola memorabilia spreads beyond North American shores, Coca-Cola trays are beginning to be discovered in other countries as well. The exact dates and origins of these foreign-language trays are often unknown.

ABOVE **Metal plate, c. 1908, 25 cm (9⅞-inch) diameter, in frame, 41 cm (16 inches) square. Imitating a fine porcelain portrait plate, this mass-produced metal "Vienna Art" plate, with its ornate frame and shadow box, was distributed to better customers. The advertising message for Coca-Cola appears in small print on the back of the plate.**

LEFT **Metal tray, 1959, 34 cm (13¼-inch) diameter. This tray is typical of a series of round Mexican trays showing Latin women engaged in a variety of activities.**

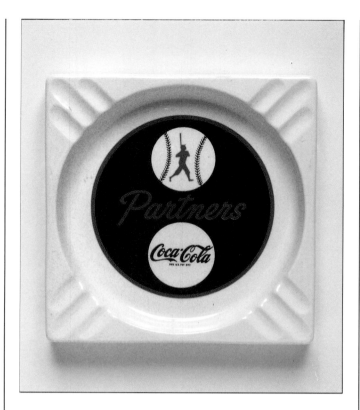

In addition to metal change trays, ceramic and glass change receivers were used to advertise Coca-Cola. Larger than a metal change tray, a change receiver was usually located near the cash register and was used, as the name implies, to give customers their change. Early examples actually carry the words "Change Receiver" and are quite rare.

In the 1920s, the Company began advertising Coca-Cola as being good with food. It was only natural that they would produce sandwich plates and other china depicting the Coca-Cola bottle and glass. The Coca-Cola Company realized the value of having the Coca-Cola trademark emblazoned on everything in sight for that moment when the customer was asked the all-important question, "What do you want to drink?" The same philosophy explains the use of ceramic, glass, Bakelite, metal and plastic ashtrays carrying the familiar Coca-Cola logo at many locations where beverages were sold, at a time when smoking was more acceptable than it is now.

BELOW **Glass change receiver, 1911, 18 cm (7-inch) diameter. Made by the Empire Ornamental Glass Company of New York, the advertising message on this change receiver is an example of reverse painting on glass.**

ABOVE **Ceramic ashtray, c. 1950, 19 cm (7½ inches) square. Baseball and Coca-Cola, long-standing "partners", were united once again in the advertising on this ashtray.**

BELOW **Ceramic plate, 1930, 21 cm (8¼-inch) diameter. The Crockery City Ice & Products Company, the local bottler in East Liverpool, Ohio, arranged** to have sandwich plates such as this one made and distributed to other bottlers throughout the country.

**BANISH
THAT YAWN**
··· bounce back to normal !

SIGNS

Signs advertising Coca-Cola have been made of a variety of materials including cloth, paper, cardboard, metal, glass, wood and plastic, and were designed for specific interior and exterior locations. Coca-Cola was heavily promoted from the outset, and the Company invested a considerable percentage of its advertising budget in signs. Not only were these signs used to decorate business establishments where Coca-Cola was sold, but they were also placed along well-travelled roads and throughout public transportation systems. Those made of cloth, paper and cardboard were less expensive to produce, less durable and meant to be replaced often. On the other hand, those made of metal, glass and wood cost more initially, but were intended to be used for longer periods of time.

CLOTH SIGNS

Signs made of oilcloth (weatherproofed canvas) were among the earliest ones used to advertise Coca-Cola. Such signs were pinned to awnings over the entrances to soda fountains and stores where Coca-Cola was sold. Lighter weight muslin signs were also produced for temporary outdoor locations such as fairs, ball games and circuses. Because they usually were meant to be seen at a distance, most cloth signs were large and had limited graphics. More detailed canvas signs were used on Coca-Cola trucks to advertise Company-sponsored radio and television shows in the 1940s and 1950s. Cloth banners, now plastic-coated, are still being used today, particularly at petrol stations and corner shops.

PAPER SIGNS

Paper signs advertising Coca-Cola have taken several forms over the years: posters or hangers, window strips and billboards. Paper posters destined for indoor use were lithographed in full colour and usually portrayed young women. From the 1890s through the early 1900s, the artwork frequently matched that used on the Company's

LEFT **Cardboard cutout, 1933, 130 cm (51¼ inches) high. An unusual advertising campaign in 1933 revolved around the concept of the refreshing** **qualities of Coca-Cola. Known as the "Banish that Yawn" series, the advertising portrayed tired people in need of a "pick-me-up".**

LEFT **Canvas sign**, *c.* 1900, 122 × 28 cm (48 × 11 inches). **This early canvas sign advertising Coca-Cola in bottles is unusual because it is smaller than most other similar signs from the period, and the trademark has an equal sign instead of a standard hyphen.**

annual calendars. Later examples showed a variety of different artworks including movie stars, food and Christmas themes. Although simply tacked to walls, many also had metal strips on the top and bottom edges and a top-centre loop for hanging, and thus were more commonly called hangers. Since hangers were sometimes shipped in mailing tubes, the weight of the metal strip at the bottom helped the poster unroll when hung, and the top strip prevented the top corners from curling.

Instead of being fastened to a wall, a paper window strip was designed to be affixed to the inside of a shop window with the printed side facing outwards. It was hoped that passers-by would see the sign, read the message and be enticed to enter the shop to buy Coca-Cola. Because such signs would fade very quickly in bright sunlight, window strips were intended for short-term use such as campaigns associated with holidays.

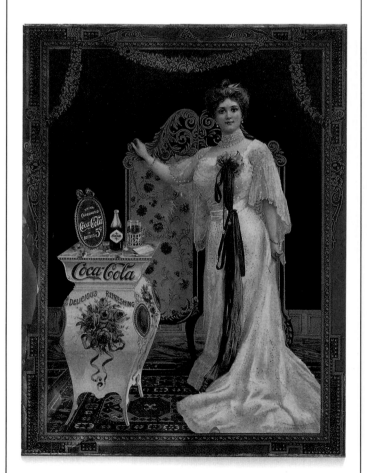

ABOVE **Paper poster, 1904, 38 × 51 cm (14⅞ × 19⅞ inches). Metropolitan Opera star Lillian Nordica lent her endorsement to Coca-Cola in 1904 and 1905. On the table are a paper-label bottle** and a note addressed to "Mme Nordica". **This is a particularly early example of standard advertising that shows the straight-sided bottle for Coca-Cola.**

ABOVE **Celluloid-covered cardboard sign, 1905, 48 × 65 cm (19 × 25¾ inches). Because this "cameo sign" featuring Lillian Nordica is covered with clear celluloid (an early plastic-like** material), it is usually called a **celluloid sign although the printing is actually on the paper underneath, not on the celluloid itself.**

ABOVE **Billboard, 1923, 6 m × 2.7 m (19 feet 8 inches × 8 feet 10 inches). Beginning in 1923, The Coca-Cola Company provided 24-sheet billboards free of charge if the bottlers paid for the advertising space. This is the first billboard provided under this plan.**

LEFT **Cardboard sign, c. 1914, 53 × 28 cm (21 × 10⅞ inches). Because numerous other companies had begun selling products similar to Coca-Cola, with similar sounding names and advertising, the Company began warning consumers about low-quality imitations. This streetcar sign cautioned people to use the full name for Coca-Cola, not current popular nicknames such as "Koke" and "Dope".**

In 1923, The Coca-Cola Company began creating 24-sheet posters which when assembled produced a billboard measuring approximately 7.6 x 3.3 m (25 x 11 feet). By 1945, the Company could boast that Coca-Cola was advertised on more billboards than any other product. Of course, once a billboard had been pasted into position, it was irretrievably lost to collectors. However, a few unused billboards are in collectors' hands, but are not easily displayed. More collectible are the numerous booklets, photos and postcards showing billboards that have been used over the years.

CARDBOARD SIGNS

Cardboard is possibly one of the most versatile materials ever used for signs. It can easily be cut to any shape desired, and unlike paper, its rigidity makes it self-supporting so it can be used for various freestanding and hanging displays. Cardboard signs with collapsible cardboard easels on the back could be used as either free-standing displays or wall signs. The Company created perhaps the most eye-catching and attractive of all Coca-Cola advertising by using die-cut cardboard. Cut by machine into unique shapes and arranged in displays, these cardboard advertising signs drew the attention of many a potential customer.

Rectangular cardboard signs have been used regularly to advertise Coca-Cola. They could be tacked up almost anywhere indoors and out. Among the earliest rectangular signs used to advertise Coca-Cola were ones placed in streetcars. Measuring approximately 53 x 28 cm (21 x 11 inches) these lightweight cardboard signs were placed in a row along the walls on either side of the streetcar's interior immediately below the ceiling line. At a time when 90% of a city's adult population rode on streetcars, this form of advertising was considered so important that the Company spent nearly one-sixth of its advertising budget on streetcar signs during the first two decades of the century. Later used on other forms of public transportation, these signs reminded weary travellers that Coca-Cola could relieve their condition.

Other rectangular signs ranged in size from a few inches square to over four feet in height. Early ones usually featured the same artwork as that used on the Company's annual calendars and trays. This artwork was directed towards drinking Coca-Cola in soda fountain settings. Later signs used especially prepared artwork showing Coca-Cola as a part of a variety of everyday situations. Since Coca-Cola advertising was changed regularly several times a year, a retailer could soon be left with walls riddled with nail holes from hanging signs. Additionally, increasing competition for wall space meant that the Coca-Cola sign might be removed prematurely and replaced by one for another product. To address both these problems, the Company in 1938 introduced corrugated cardboard frames into which standard-sized cardboard signs could be inserted. Besides requiring only one or two nails, these frames secured a permanent location in the store for Coca-Cola advertising.

As this advertising strategy matured, the Company in 1941 replaced the cardboard frames with ones made of wood and metal finished in a bright metallic gold colour.

ABOVE **Cardboard sign, 1942, in frame, 57 × 82 cm (22¼ × 32¼ inches). War-era advertising didn't ignore women in uniform,** as demonstrated by this framed cardboard sign of an Army Nurse stepping off an aeroplane.

RIGHT **Cardboard sign, c. 1955, 41 × 68 cm (15⅞ × 26¾ inches). As Coca-Cola gained in international popularity, native people began to appear in the advertising, such as the Oriental woman on this sign for use in** Hong Kong. The Chinese version of the Coca-Cola trademark is a phonetic rendering which when translated reads, "permit mouth to be able to rejoice".

The cardboard inserts, as they were now called, were changed three times a year in January, May and September. This practice continued into the 1960s, but the wooden and later aluminum frames were no longer marked Coca-Cola. Since these framed cardboard signs were in widespread use when they were growing up, Coca-Cola collectors from the "Baby Boomer" generation are particularly fond of such signs. These signs were used worldwide as Coca-Cola truly became an international beverage recognized everywhere. Today, the value of these cardboard signs is much more a function of the artwork shown than the language used.

In addition to rectangular cardboard signs, Coca-Cola has also been heavily advertised with irregular-shaped die-cut cardboard signs. Although thousands of different die-cut signs have been produced over the years, they fall into three main categories: cutouts, festoons and multipiece displays. Considered to be among the most attractive Coca-Cola collectibles, many die-cut cardboard signs were also embossed or three-dimensional, further adding to their charm. This form of advertising for Coca-Cola is still being used today, additional testament to its enduring effectiveness.

When used by collectors, the term "cutout" usually refers to a single lithographed piece of die-cut cardboard, either freestanding or hanging. The majority of cutouts portrayed people, most frequently women, at leisure. Although many different subjects were used for the

LEFT **Cardboard cutout, 1910, 100 cm (39½ inches) high. Called "Man on the Grass", this cutout is one of the few early examples of advertising for Coca-Cola that show men instead of the more traditional pretty young women.**

CARDBOARD CUTOUTS

BELOW **Cardboard cutout, 1924, 102 cm (40 inches) high. During the first few decades of the century, the Company used the same "Coca-Cola Girl" on a** variety of advertising items for a particular year. The girl shown here was also used on trays and calendars in 1924.

ABOVE **Cardboard cutout, 1927, 100 cm (39½ inches) high. During the 1920s and 1930s, many cutouts became more elaborate, often consisting of several pieces.** The addition of an actual working paper parasol gave this cutout a three-dimensional, more life-like quality.

LEFT **Cardboard cutout, 1922, 82 cm (32¼ inches) high. This three-fold display shows a young woman in a typical swimsuit of the time riding an "aquaplane", a surfboard-like device towed by a motorboat.**

ABOVE **Cardboard cutout, 1934, 67 cm (26⅜ inches) high. Beginning in 1931 and continuing into the 1960s, artist Haddon Sundblom prepared a different Santa artwork each year, which was then used for magazine ads, posters and cutouts such as this one.**

RIGHT **Cardboard cutout, 1935, 93 cm (36½ inches) high. The Coca-Cola Company frequently employed the services of the foremost illustrators of the day. Norman Rockwell painted the charming artwork that was used for this cutout as well as the 1935 calendar.**

artwork, certain general trends are evident: soda fountain customers in the 1910s, bathing beauties in the 1920s, movie stars in the 1930s, military personnel in the 1940s. Starting in the mid-1920s, Coca-Cola with food was also a frequent subject. Beginning in 1931, The Coca-Cola Company began issuing Santa Claus cutouts at Christmas time, a practice that continues to this day.

A festoon is a set of die-cut cardboard signs designed to hang as a unit from a wall or soda fountain backbar. Shortly after the turn of the century, the first festoons were nothing more than a series of pieces of die-cut cardboad strung together to spell out the word "Coca-Cola" one letter at a time. Soon festoons became colourful affairs, typically showing attractive women surrounded by a profusion of flowers. Starting in the 1940s, the subject matter was expanded to include warships, planes, trees, birds, cars, gemstones and teenagers.

In an attempt to dominate shopfront windows, The Coca-Cola Company devised multipiece sets of die-cut cardboard signs capable of spanning an entire window.

ABOVE **Cardboard cutout, 1954, 65 × 88 cm (25⅜ × 34½ inches). The elfin creature shown on this cutout was called "Sprite". Used throughout the 1940s and 1950s,** he wore a soda jerk's hat when promoting fountain Coca-Cola, but a bottle-cap hat when advertising bottled Coca-Cola.

ABOVE **Cardboard cutout, 1937, 156 cm (61½ inches) high. Smartly dressed in his sparkling white uniform and garrison cap, the waiter in a soda fountain was commonly referred to as a "soda jerk" (because of the jerking action used to pull the lever on a soda dispenser).**

RIGHT **Cardboard cutout, 1953, 30 × 38 cm (11⅞ × 14⅞ inches). In the early 1950s, The Coca-Cola Company began a concentrated effort to produce special advertising directed toward the "Negro market". African-American figures, such as accordionist Graham Jackson shown here, were recruited to endorse Coca-Cola.**

FESTOONS

TOP **Cardboard festoon, 1929, 2.4 m (8 feet) wide. Because they were made of several individual pieces of cardboard, later festoons could be adapted to the space available. The "Orchid Festoon" shown here used multicoloured satin ribbons to connect the pieces.**

ABOVE **Cardboard festoon, c. 1910, 145 cm (57 inches) wide. The earliest festoons for Coca-Cola were made of several pieces of die-cut cardboard fastened together with grommets. When it was tacked to the backbar, the end pieces hung down naturally under their own weight.**

These easily erected displays were readily accepted by shop owners who wanted to make their shops look attractive and inviting to passers-by. Because the pieces were separate, they could be set up to create a three-dimensional effect, adding not only breadth to the visual display but depth as well. The use of these displays reached their zenith in the period from the late 1920s through the 1930s, when as many as twenty separate pieces were used to create one display.

METAL SIGNS

Although most metal signs were designed exclusively for outdoor use because of their durability, some were intended specifically for indoors and others for either location. Metal signs were manufactured in all sizes, shapes and designs so that they could be used in a variety of places. Outdoor signs tended to be fairly simple with few colours and graphics so they could be read at a distance and their message quickly grasped. By contrast, indoor signs would be seen more closely and for a longer period of time. Consequently they were usually more elaborate in design and used more colours and detailed graphics to convey the message. To justify their higher cost, metal signs were intended to remain in place, whether indoors or out, for a longer period of time than either cloth, paper or cardboard signs.

Some outdoor signs were made of thin tin-plated metal with a lithographed finish, while others meant for extended use were made of heavy metal with a porcelain enamel finish. The thin metal signs usually had no holes for hanging and were called tacker signs because they were installed by nailing right through the metal to attach them to walls and fences. Porcelain signs came with pre-drilled holes, grommets or brackets for hanging. Starting in the 1920s, signs were designed with special frames and poles

ABOVE **Metal sign, c. 1903, 22 × 27 cm (8⅜ × 10⅜ inches). This oval sign may be the first metal sign to feature the straight-sided, paper-label bottle for Coca-Cola.**

BELOW **Cardboard display, 1929, 71 cm (28 inches) high. Made of seventeen individual pieces, the "Circus Window Display" was quite an impressive sight when it was set up in a store window. Stores using the circus window display were also provided with miniature versions for children to cut out at home.**

ABOVE **Metal sign, c. 1910, 90 ×
29 cm (35½ × 11⅝ inches). The
paper-label bottle was used not
just in the United States, but
throughout the rest of the world
as well, as evidenced by this
French language tacker sign.**

LEFT **Metal sign, 1933, 69 × 48 cm
(27 × 19 inches). The bottle on
this sign is commonly called the
Christmas bottle because of the
25 December, 1923, patent date
on the bottle. This is the bottle
shown on most Coca-Cola
advertising items from the 1920s
and 1930s.**

ABOVE **Metal sign, 1927, 76 × 20
cm (30 × 7¾ inches). This two-
sided arrow sign originally hung**
from a wrought-iron bracket
fastened at right angles to a wall,
pointing the way to refreshment.

ABOVE **Metal sign, 1954, 48 cm (19 inches) wide. Twelve-bottle cartons, such as the one shown on this die-cut sign, were used on an experimental basis by some bottlers in the mid-1950s.**

BELOW **Metal sign, 1927, 28 × 20 cm (11⅛ × 8⅛ inches). This small sign is a rare example of the Coca-Cola trademark being partially obscured in the artwork. So well-known was the trademark that anyone who saw this sign would have instantly recognized that it advertised Coca-Cola.**

so that they could stand alone outside shops as well as along well-travelled thoroughfares. The Company also made two-sided flange signs which attached to buildings at right angles so that potential customers could view the signs from both directions. For some business establishments, the Company produced large signs that carried the name of the business in addition to an advertisement for Coca-Cola.

Indoor metal signs were generally smaller than their outdoor counterparts. Many were lithographed in full colour to enhance not only the attractiveness of the advertising, but the interior of the shop as well. The artwork was frequently pictorial, showing attractive women along with glasses or bottles of Coca-Cola. Many indoor signs were self-framed, meaning that they were formed by stamping the sign and the frame from the same sheet of metal. When such signs featured a pretty young woman, the added frame elevated the sign to the status of a work of art. Because of their eye-catching appeal, these signs usually remained hanging until replaced by Company representatives.

BELOW **Metal sign, 1970, 39 × 56 cm (15⅝ × 21⅞ inches). Made in Mexico, this self-framed sign** with photographic artwork shows that pretty girls could still sell Coca-Cola in the 1970s.

COCA-COLA
MARCA REGISTRADA

COCA-COLA
refresca en grande

TOME
Coca-Cola

GLASS SIGNS

Glass signs were made by printing the advertising message in reverse on the back side of a piece of glass. When viewed from the front, the message showed through the glass correctly. Such signs are usually called reverse painting on glass. The effect of the clean glass with its sparkling qualities made the sign seem more vibrant than a cardboard or metal sign.

Glass signs with Coca-Cola advertising first appeared around 1900. The earliest known examples are oval or round and carry the "Drink Coca-Cola 5¢" message with no pictorial graphics. They were ordinarily hung by attached metal chains. Later, thick, rectangular, beveled glass signs carried the message to "Drink Coca-Cola". In the 1920s, round glass signs were designed to be glued directly to mirrored walls and backbars in drug stores and soda fountains. In the 1930s, Art Deco reverse-painted glass signs were available for upscale locations. The use of this type of glass sign ended by the 1950s, replaced by self-contained electric light-up fixtures with glass panels.

BELOW **Glass sign, 1933, 72 × 30 cm (28¼ × 11¾ inches). With its wooden embellishments, this black and silver reverse-painted glass sign epitomizes the Art Deco style.**

ABOVE **Wood and metal sign, 1937, 60 × 58 cm (23½ × 23 inches). Made of plywood with applied three-dimensional metal trim, this sign is an excellent example of signs manufactured by Kay Displays, Inc.**

BELOW **Wooden menu sign, 1940, 35 × 69 cm (13¾ × 27¼ inches). With its low prices and unusual food choices, this artifact gives insight into a typical luncheonette menu of the 1940s.**

WOODEN SIGNS

Beginning in 1933 and continuing into the 1950s, the Company used mass-produced wooden signs for indoor use. The wood used was actually plywood or chipboard made from compressed wood fibres. In fact, most of these signs were not made exclusively of wood, but had embellishments made of other materials including metal, plaster, rope, cloth and plastic. These added a three-dimensional quality, thereby increasing the attractiveness of the signs. Virtually all of these signs were made by the advertising specialty firm Kay Displays, Inc. Because of their extensive variety and good quality, the signs produced by this company form a fascinating collection in their own right.

In addition to Kay Displays' signs, chipboard was also used for outdoor signs during World War II. Because of the war effort, metal was in short supply, and chipboard served as a temporary replacement. There are a number of instances where the artwork used on chipboard signs was the same as that previously used on metal signs.

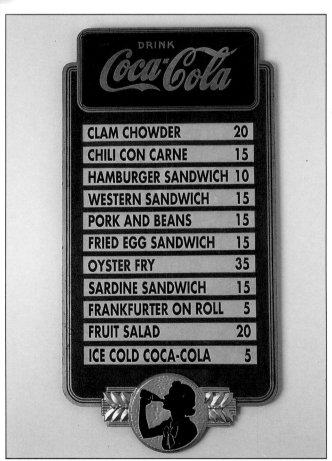

DRINK *Coca-Cola*

CLAM CHOWDER	20
CHILI CON CARNE	15
HAMBURGER SANDWICH	10
WESTERN SANDWICH	15
PORK AND BEANS	15
FRIED EGG SANDWICH	15
OYSTER FRY	35
SARDINE SANDWICH	15
FRANKFURTER ON ROLL	5
FRUIT SALAD	20
ICE COLD COCA-COLA	5

THERMOMETER

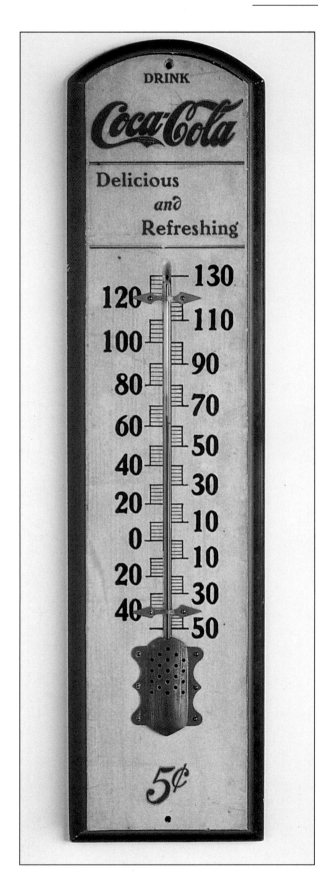

LEFT **Wooden thermometer, c. 1920, 13 × 53 cm (5⅛ × 20⅞ inches). Because of its usefulness, this thermometer would have remained in place long after other advertising items had been discarded.**

ABOVE **Metal thermometer, 1941, 18 × 40 cm (6⅞ × 15¾ inches). With its Art Deco design, this thermometer would have complemented the design of up-to-date drug stores and soda fountains in the 1940s.**

SPECIAL USE SIGNS

The advertising for Coca-Cola served a secondary purpose on some signs. The primary purpose was utilitarian. Thermometers, menu boards, chalkboards, "Push" and "Pull" door signs, and door push bars are examples of such signs.

Thermometers were manufactured in wood well into the 1920s, then in metal starting in the 1920s, in chipboard during World War II, and finally in plastic starting in the 1960s. Wall-mounted menu boards were manufactured by Kay Displays, primarily of wood. Slotted channels were used to insert strips preprinted with food choices and prices. Chalkboards, made of cardboard or metal, served the same purpose as menu boards, but allowed the daily "specials" to be easily changed. Door signs reminded patrons about Coca-Cola as they entered restaurants and shops where they might order a glass or bottle of Coca-Cola.

BELOW **Plastic sign, c. 1962, 35 × 23 cm (13¾ × 9¼ inches). Unlike earlier signs that were constructed from several** **materials, many modern signs are made from moulded plastic to achieve the same three-dimensional effect.**

ABOVE **Metal chalkboard, 1940, 49 × 69 cm (19¼ × 27 inches). Chalkboards with Coca-Cola advertising have been distributed to food retailers since the 1920s. The artwork in the lower right corner of this one is called the "Silhouette Girl" logo.**

LIGHTING FIXTURES AND LIGHTED SIGNS

CHAPTER 9

Of all the items that have been used to advertise Coca-Cola over the years, perhaps none are so captivating as the lighting fixtures used to illuminate soda fountains and drug stores. Beginning soon after the turn of the century and continuing for thirty years or so, the Company provided shop owners with items that were not only advertisements for Coca-Cola, but useful lighting fixtures as well. Though they were not particularly expensive at the time, such a seemingly generous gift was highly treasured – to the extent that a few lighting fixtures have remained hanging in the original stores to this day.

The earliest known lighting fixtures to advertise Coca-Cola were made of leaded or mosaic glass. Rectangular in shape, these fixtures were intended to hang over a soda fountain or in a window display. It was suggested in Company literature that retailers be encouraged to keep such lights turned on at night after business hours as a security measure, but also to make it clear where Coca-Cola could be purchased during the day. Company records indicate that the Pike Stained Glass Company made the leaded glass "chandeliers" only in 1911, and that the Pittsburgh Mosaic Glass Company produced similar fixtures from 1911 to at least 1913.

The next lighting fixtures to advertise Coca-Cola were spherical. There are two versions of the leaded glass "ball" shade: one designed to hang from the ceiling and the other to sit atop dispensing units. A 1917 photograph shows that one retailer actually used a ball shade to replace the glass globe in a street light at the curb outside his drug store. These lights have been reproduced in small quantities, but without the curved glass of the originals.

The 1920s saw the first use of two more leaded glass lighting fixtures advertising Coca-Cola. The first was a traditional-shaped leaded glass shade, equipped with a chain for hanging. Constructed of red, green, and white glass, this shade has as its distinguishing feature the following wording stamped into the metal band separating the "crown" from the body of the shade: "Property of The Coca-Cola Company to be returned on demand." Since this fixture was issued for a number of years, there are several variations, including more recent reproductions.

LEFT **Glass light with metal base, c. 1929, 51 cm (20 inches) high. This oversized replica of a hobbleskirt bottle has a built-in** mechanism that could be set so that the light could blink off and on at an adjustable rate.

LEFT **Leaded glass chandelier, 1911, 65 cm (25½ inches) long. As an example of the long-lasting appeal of such fixtures, this particular one-of-a-kind rectangular light remained hanging in the same shop for over fifty years.**

LEFT **Leaded glass light, c. 1915, 29 cm (11½-inch) diameter, on marble base, 91 cm (36 inches) high overall. After Coca-Cola had been measured into a glass, carbonated water was drawn from one of the unit's three spigots. Although such dispensing units were standard fixtures in early soda fountains, the addition of a Coca-Cola ball shade transformed this one into an advertisement for Coca-Cola.**

RIGHT **Leaded glass light, c. 1920, 91 cm (36 inches) high. Made by the Metropolitan Art Glass Company of New York, this giant illuminated hobbleskirt bottle was used both indoors and out to advertise Coca-Cola.**

LEFT **Glass lighted sign, c. 1938, 34 cm (13½ inches) high. The bottle shown on the curved glass of this lighted counter sign carries the designation "D 105529", indicating the design patent number assigned to the shape of the bottle in 1937.**

ABOVE **Glass sign with metal framework, c. 1925, 66 × 29 cm (26 × 11⅝ inches). The red, green, and yellow colour combination on this brass-framed sign is typical of 1920s Coca-Cola advertising.**

The second leaded glass item introduced in the 1920s was a three-foot high replica of the hobbleskirt bottle. Because of its higher cost, this fixture was usually reserved for the bottler's own use at the bottling plant as well as for special displays elsewhere.

By the mid-1920s, milk-glass shades began to replace leaded glass fixtures. Made of a single piece of moulded glass, the first of these shades had Coca-Cola printed in red along with green pinstriping. A brass tassel hanging from the bottom and a brass fitter attached to the top completed the unit. Less ornate milk-glass shades were used throughout the 1930s. These later examples were made in a variety of sizes, ranging from 25 to 41 cm (10 to 16 inches) in diameter. Whereas the earlier leaded glass fixtures had been designed primarily for decoration, the milk-glass shades were truly meant to light an area. In fact, bottlers used them in the offices and workrooms of their own plants.

Unlike lighting fixtures, lighted signs were not really intended to light up anything except themselves. Such signs have been made continuously from the 1910s. Depending on their intended use, lighted signs were designed either to be fastened to the wall, hung from the ceiling, or set on horizontal surfaces such as worktops. In addition to the Coca-Cola trademark, these signs often included messages such as "Serve Yourself", "Please Pay Cashier" and "Please Pay When Served". Some had clocks built into them. Because of these additional attributes, these signs usually remained in place longer than ordinary signs would have.

While early lighted signs were made of glass, most examples since the 1960s have been made of plastic. Most lighted signs were illuminated by ordinary incandescent or florescent light bulbs. Neon tubing was also used to light some signs and clocks as early as the 1930s. Some examples even had the neon tubing bent into the shape of the Coca-Cola trademark.

BELOW **Milk-glass light with metal tassel, c. 1929, 34 cm (13½-inch) diameter. At a cost of £5.30 ($8) each from the Progress Gas** **Fixture Company of New York, lighting fixtures such as this one were used in soda fountains and bottling plants.**

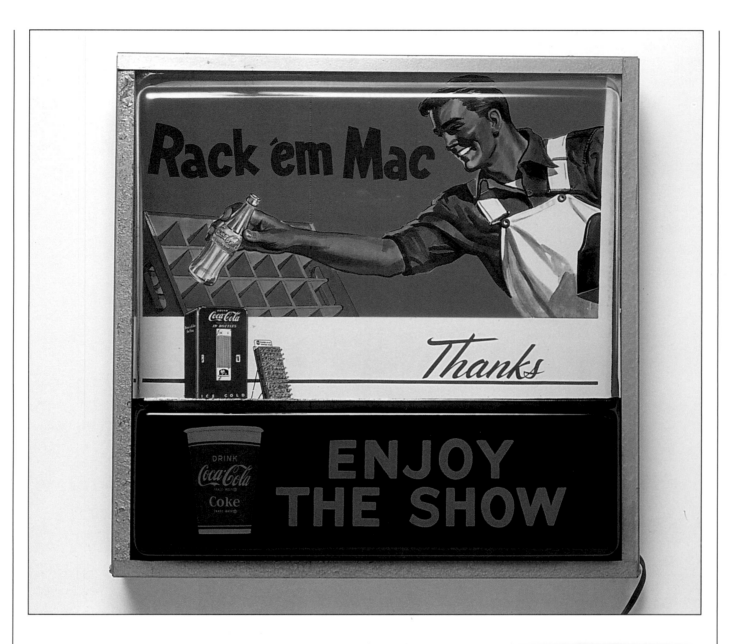

ABOVE **Metal and plastic lighted sign, c. 1950, 39 cm (15½ inches) square. Signs such as this one were used to remind customers to place their empty bottles in the rack next to the vending machine.**

RIGHT **Neon sign, 1988, 50 × 44 cm (19¾ × 17¼ inches). This neon sign was used by the Coca-Cola bottler in Philadelphia, home of the Liberty Bell.**

CLOCKS

As a category, clocks comprise one of the more expensive but enduring forms of advertising used for Coca-Cola. As early as the 1890s, The Coca-Cola Company saw the value of having permanent advertising that promoted the sale of Coca-Cola. While most other advertising was expected to last for less than a year, clocks were meant to last indefinitely, thereby justifying their higher initial cost.

The first clocks to advertise Coca-Cola were made by the Baird Clock Company of Plattsburgh, New York. Initially in 1893, they cost the Company £1.83 ($2.75) each and were given as premiums to dealers who bought 228 l (50 gallons) of Coca-Cola syrup in a year. Baird clocks, key-wound and pendulum-driven, had large round faces with Roman numerals. Frequently called a "figure-eight" clock, the standard Baird clock had two round doors – one over the face and the other over the pendulum – that were made of moulded composition, a combination of sawdust, wood fibres and glue. The raised lettering on the surface of the upper door carried the advertising slogan, "Coca-Cola, The Ideal Brain Tonic", used from 1893 through 1897. The slogans on the smaller lower door varied over the years and included such phrases as "Delightful Beverage", "Specific for Headache", "Relieves Mental & Physical Exhaustion", "5¢", "Relieves Exhaustion", "Delicious" and "Refreshing". Baird also made "gallery" versions of these "Brain Tonic" clocks that were round and merely looked like the top of the clocks described above, but without the pendulum and lower door portion. A later Baird clock carried the advertising on metal panel inserts. Even though a remarkable number of these clocks from the 1890s have survived, they have always been highly sought after and hence expensive to acquire. These early clocks have been reproduced in recent times.

The next type of clock used to advertise Coca-Cola is commonly called a schoolhouse clock. The upper portion was octagonal in shape and made of finished wood surrounding a glass-covered, circular face. The lower portion consisted of a wood and glass door covering a

LEFT **Pendulum clock, 1911, 100 cm (39½ inches) high. Because the woman portrayed on the lower panel is reminiscent of the** artwork of illustrator Charles Dana Gibson, this Gilbert clock is commonly called the "Gibson Girl" clock.

LEFT **Pendulum clock, c. 1895, 79 cm (31 inches) high. This particular example of a "figure-eight" Baird clock does not appear to have been refinished as was the custom for such composition clocks when they started to show signs of wear.**

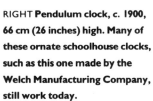

RIGHT **Pendulum clock, c. 1900, 66 cm (26 inches) high. Many of these ornate schoolhouse clocks, such as this one made by the Welch Manufacturing Company, still work today.**

compartment for the pendulum. Unlike a Baird clock, the advertising message was printed on a schoolhouse clock's face in red. Occasionally these clocks are found with Coca-Cola artwork, lithographed on cardboard, inserted in the case behind the pendulum. Schoolhouse clocks advertising Coca-Cola were made first by the Welch Manufacturing Company around the turn of the century and later by the Ingraham Company.

In about 1905, The Coca-Cola Company began distributing large rectangular clocks, commonly called regulator clocks. This type of clock had a wooden case with a single door consisting of two framed pieces of glass.

Once again, the face carried the advertising for Coca-Cola printed in red. Using the same face as on the earlier schoolhouse clocks, Ingraham produced this kind of clock through 1910. Beginning in 1911, The Coca-Cola Company turned to the Gilbert Clock Corporation to produce regulators. Several changes were made at this point: the advertising on the face was simplified to "Drink Coca-Cola", the numerals were changed from Roman to Arabic,

and advertising was added to the lower glass panel. These rectangular clocks were available through the 1930s, but were gradually replaced by electric clocks. Until these clocks were discontinued in 1941, Gilbert made many changes to the wooden case as well as the advertising message.

Electric clocks advertising Coca-Cola began to appear in the early 1930s. They could be used in more locations

ABOVE **Electric clock, 1948, 91 cm (36 inches) wide. This deluxe clock with ornamental rings and background panel made by Kay Displays, Inc., was intended for high-quality establishments.**

LEFT **Electric clock, 1940, 46 cm (18¼ inches) square. Besides drawing attention to the clock itself, the neon tubing surrounding the face was intended to help illuminate the shop's interior at night after business hours.**

because they were smaller and didn't need to be wound. The advertising usually appeared either on the face of the clock or on the glass covering the face. At first the cases were made of wood and metal. Plastic cases and faces began to appear in the late 1950s. Starting in the late 1930s, some clocks were illuminated with either neon or ordinary light bulbs. After World War II, as electric clocks became less expensive, clocks were used much more extensively to advertise Coca-Cola. As a result, there are many styles and variations of clocks, made by dozens of manufacturers. The slogans and graphics, as well as the materials and design, help collectors date these myriad clocks.

In addition to these wall clocks, The Coca-Cola Company and its local bottlers also distributed table and desk clocks. Among the earliest of these, dating from around 1910, are clocks with leather-covered cases with the advertising appearing in gold-stamped lettering.

ABOVE **Electric clock, c. 1963, 41 cm (16 inches) square. With its all-plastic case illuminated from** inside by a ring-shaped florescent bulb, this clock carries the "things go better with Coke" logo.

DESK CLOCKS

ABOVE **Wind-up clock, c. 1935, 10 × 8 cm (4 × 3 inches). When this desk clock is running, the "Drink Coca-Cola • Ice Cold" slogan rotates constantly in the small semicircular window at the bottom of the dial.**

LEFT **Wind-up clock, c. 1910, 9 cm (3⅜ inches) square. Decorated with gold leaf lettering, leather desk clocks such as the one shown here were distributed from 1905 to 1915.**

TOYS AND GAMES

For some collectors, toys and games are the most beloved Coca-Cola collectibles. Until the Company instituted a licensing program in the 1980s, toy manufacturers in many countries produced countless toys with the Coca-Cola trademark, but without the Company's involvement. However, the Company did produce such things as playing cards and games to promote the sale of Coca-Cola.

In the days before customers paid a deposit on bottles, bottlers needed some way to encourage the return of empty bottles. Some local bottlers developed premium plans to accomplish this goal. When customers returned empty bottles to stores, they were given coupons indicating the number of bottles returned. After amassing a sufficient number of coupons, the customer could then visit the bottler and exchange the coupons for useful "gifts". These premiums were usually nothing more than readily available household items. Other bottlers, in an obvious effort to increase sales, merely offered the same premiums in exchange for bottle caps. In both cases, among the most popular of these premiums were mass-produced toys to which the bottlers simply added the Coca-Cola logo.

The Coca-Cola bottler in St Louis, Missouri, probably led all others in the distribution of these toys in the 1920s and 1930s. Vintage photographs of his special premium room show scooters, bicycles, dolls, play cookers, wagons, lanterns, etc. It is probably not a coincidence that the first Coca-Cola toy trucks were manufactured by The Metalcraft Corporation, also located in St Louis.

In the first three decades of the century, Coca-Cola bottlers sporadically distributed playing cards featuring the same artwork used on other items. In the 1930s and 1940s, the Company and its bottlers took advantage of the card playing craze then sweeping the nation by distributing numerous decks of playing cards advertising Coca-Cola. Distributing Coca-Cola playing cards has been a standard advertising practice since that time. While collectors prefer complete decks in original boxes, there are decks so difficult to obtain in this form that some collectors have settled for single playing cards.

LEFT **Cardboard whistle, c. 1910, 4 × 16 cm (1¾ × 6¼ inches). Featuring the straight-sided, paper-label bottle, this whistle produces a high-pitched, kazoo-like sound when blown.**

ABOVE **Metal train, c. 1930, 76 cm (30 inches) long. This key-wound American Flyer train was probably ordered by the St Louis, Missouri, bottler to be used as a premium.**

RIGHT **Metal train car, c. 1930, 15 cm (5⅞ inches) long. Each car of this American Flyer train carried Coca-Cola advertising on its roof.**

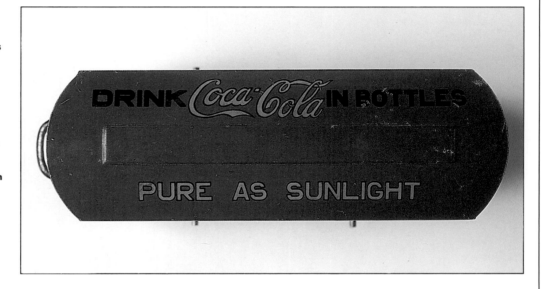

LEFT **Metal truck, 1931, 28 cm (11 inches) long. Made by The Metalcraft Corporation of St Louis, Missouri, this immensely popular, miniature A-frame Coca-Cola truck was sold in department stores and mail-order catalogs at a cost of about 30p (50¢) each.**

PLAYING CARDS

ABOVE **Playing cards, c. 1940, 6 × 9 cm (2¼ × 3½ inches). Made by the Atlantic Playing Card Company, these cards show the familiar "Silhouette Girl" logo.**

RIGHT **Playing cards, 1915, 6 × 9 cm (2½ × 3½ inches). These cards, showing the "Elaine" artwork from the 1915 Coca-Cola calendar, could be ordered from the Western Coca-Cola Bottling Company for 16p (25¢).**

ABOVE **Boxed game, 1949, 23 × 8 × 4 cm (9¼ × 3¼ × 1¾ inches). The object of this "Tower of** Hannoi" game was to move the eight circular disks from one peg to another by following rules.

Beginning in the early 1940s and continuing into the 1960s, the Company produced a series of games, manufactured by the Milton Bradley Company of Springfield, Massachusetts. These games were usually packaged in red boxes. The list of games includes anagrams, backgammon, bingo, draughts, chess, cribbage, darts, dominoes, ring toss, noughts and crosses and wall quoits. These games were typically distributed to schools, churches, clubs and hospitals. During World War II, the Company and the bottlers also distributed these games to military bases in the US and abroad.

Another category of items frequently thought of as toys are miniatures, small-sized replicas of larger items. For Coca-Cola, miniatures included bottles, cartons, cases, cooler boxes, dispensers and glasses. It was not surprising that The Coca-Cola Company distributed miniature versions of its own merchandising items, thereby enabling children to play at being Coca-Cola customers and dealers. Toy manufacturers have also made toy cooler dispensers, some of which double as savings banks.

ABOVE **Plastic bank, c. 1948, 14 cm (5⅜ inches) high. A miniature replica of a Vendo V-83 machine,** this toy bank dispensed a miniature Coca-Cola bottle when a coin was inserted.

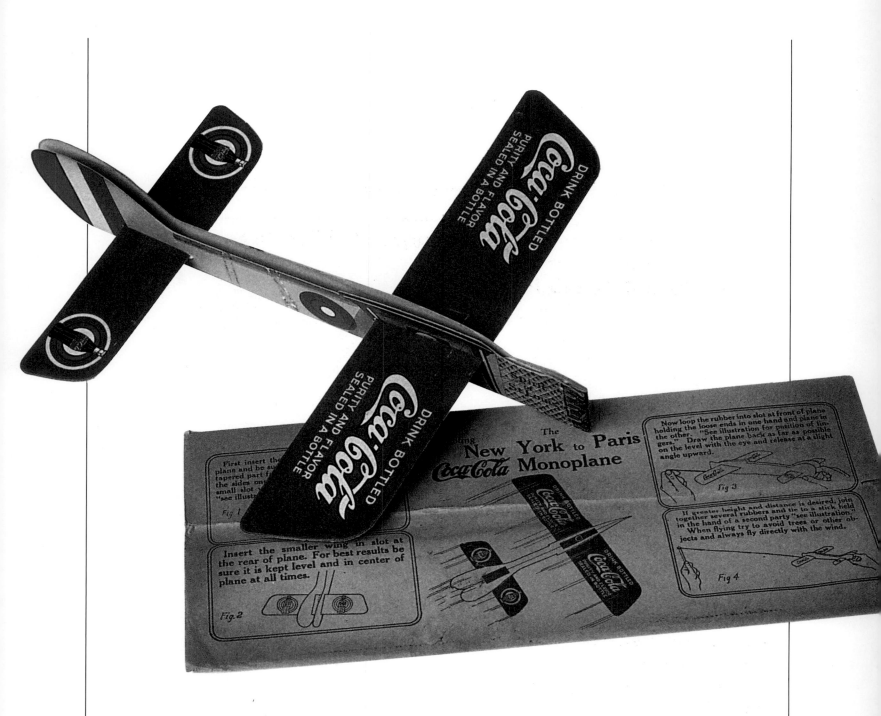

Toys and games form such an eclectic group of objects that it is difficult to generalize about them. Toy trucks and other vehicles traditionally form the foundation for most collections of Coca-Cola toys. The list of Coca-Cola toys is seemingly endless and includes bang guns, clickers, jump ropes, kites, marbles, puzzles, spinning tops, toy aeroplanes, toy robots and whistles. Since most of these toys were produced without the knowledge or permission of The Coca-Cola Company, there is little information about exactly what was produced and when. For this reason, perhaps no other area of Coca-Cola collecting is as exciting as this one, since previously unknown toys are constantly being discovered.

ABOVE **Cardboard aeroplane, c. 1928, 25 cm (10 inches) long. Coca-Cola celebrated Charles Lindbergh's 1927 trans-Atlantic flight with the distribution of this replica glider of his "Spirit of St Louis" plane.**

ABOVE **Metal bus, c. 1955, 10 cm (3¾ inches) long, bus terminal, 15 cm (6 inches long), and track, 108 cm (42½ inches) long. Made for the American market by German toy manufacturer Technofix,** this key-wound, two-piece double-decker bus travels back and forth on a straight track, alternately dropping off and picking up its upper deck with each pass through the terminal.

BELOW **Plastic truck, 1949, 28 cm (11 inches) long.** This toy truck, made by Louis Marx & Company of New York, is a fairly faithful representation of the gull-wing trucks then being used by many Coca-Cola bottlers.

ABOVE **Plastic cooler box, c. 1950, 14 × 10 × 13 cm (5⅜ × 4 × 5⅛ inches).** This miniature picnic cooler box came complete with clear plastic ice and two 10 cm (3½-inch) high plastic Coca-Cola bottles.

NOVELTIES

One of the most popular, personal and inexpensive forms of advertising has been novelties, small useful items that consumers of Coca-Cola would invariably carry with them. Records show for example that from 1906 to 1913, the Company made the following expenditures for novelties: more than £60,000 ($90,000) for leather novelties; £20,000 ($30,000) for celluloid novelties; £16,666 ($25,000) for matches; £10,000 ($15,000) for pocketknives; £20,000 ($30,000) for watch fobs; and £26,666 ($40,000) for fans. Each item cost mere pennies, so the number of such items distributed is staggering.

Leather novelties included wallets, coin purses, match safes and pocket notebooks. The advertising on the leather was usually imprinted using gold leaf. Wallets and coin purses were issued from early in the century to the present time. Before the advent of safety matches, a match safe was used to enclose a book of matches so that they wouldn't accidentally ignite in a person's pocket. In addition to having blank pages for personal notes, leather-covered notebooks advertising Coca-Cola usually carried a listing of how much syrup each retailer had used in the previous year.

Made from cellulose (a wood fibre derivative), celluloid was an early forerunner of plastic. A thin sheet of transparent celluloid could be used to cover the paper portion of an advertising item printed in full colour, thereby increasing that item's durability. Additionally, advertising objects could be made from non-transparent celluloid by printing directly on the celluloid itself. Celluloid-covered items advertising Coca-Cola included signs, pocket mirrors, watch fobs and cuff links, while items made entirely of celluloid included bookmarks, pocketknife handles, and covers for pocket notebooks, stamp holders and blotter pads.

Judging by surviving examples, the use of book matches to advertise Coca-Cola began shortly after the turn of the century. Since matchbooks were disposable items, relatively few examples were saved. Those that have survived testify to the wide variety of cover designs that were used in the early years. Girls, straight-sided

LEFT **Key and ring, 1959, 11 cm (4½ inches) long. In a clever pun, the reverse side of this automobile key says, "Steady promotion is the key to sales".**

RIGHT **Leather wallet, c. 1920, 21 × 10 cm (8¼ × 3⅝ inches). Produced at a time when the United States was changing to smaller-sized currency, this pigskin wallet has compartments for both the "old" and "new" bills.**

ABOVE **Leather coin purse, c. 1910, 6 × 7 cm (2½ × 2¾ inches). With gold-leaf stamping, more-expensive novelties such as this one were generally given to shop clerks in order to build product loyalty.**

bottles and diamond-shaped bottle labels were the most common subjects. In addition to the advertising on the cover, it was not unusual for early matchbooks to have advertising slogans on each individual match. Before World War I, several different designs were used each year. After that time, the Company employed fewer designs, often using the same artwork for several years in a row. Since the late 1920s, bottlers have frequently shared the advertising space on the cover with local businesses that sold Coca-Cola. There were also matches made to commemorate special events.

ABOVE **Leather match safe, 1906, 4 × 6 cm (1¾ × 2⅜ inches). The Coca-Cola Company often took part in trade conventions such as those held by the National Association of Retail Druggists [chemists] (NARD).**

ABOVE **Pocket mirror, c. 1908, 5 cm (2⅛-inch) diameter. Pre-1916 pocket mirrors issued by The Coca-Cola Company promoted fountain Coca-Cola,** so some bottlers, such as the one in Tuscaloosa, Alabama, had their own mirrors produced to advertise bottled Coca-Cola.

ABOVE **Pocket mirror, 1914, 4 × 7 cm (1¾ × 2¾ inches). The artwork on Company-issued pocket mirrors was usually the same as that on the annual Coca-Cola calendar and other items. This mirror is unusual in that the only other item to carry the same artwork is a 1914 magazine ad.**

LEFT **Match books, c. 1912, 4 × 5 cm (1⅝ × 2⅛ inches) each. This pair of match books exemplifies how the same artwork was adapted for both bottle and fountain sales.**

LEFT **Metal pocketknife, c. 1910, 10 cm (3⅜ inches) long. With its built-in bottle opener, this pocketknife was an ideal give-away for Coca-Cola bottlers.**

ABOVE **Metal watch fob, c. 1910, 4 × 4 cm (1⅜ × 1½ inches). From about 1908 to 11912, the swastika was recognized the world over as a good-luck symbol.**

Pocketknives have also been a popular Coca-Cola giveaway since the turn of the century. In addition to the blades, some pocketknives also had bottle openers and corkscrews. Most Coca-Cola pocketknives were distributed by local bottlers, some of whom added their name to the advertising for Coca-Cola. Although more expensive than most novelties, pocketknives were appreciated by the men and boys who received them.

Made of celluloid or metal, or a combination of both, a watch fob was attached by a leather strap to a pocket watch. The fob hung out of a man's pocket so that when he wanted to know the time, a pull on the fob would bring out his pocket watch. Although there are many different examples of watch fobs advertising Coca-Cola, they were used for a relatively short period beginning about 1905. After World War I the increasing popularity of wrist watches reduced the necessity for watch fobs, and they were eventually phased out as an advertising novelty for Coca-Cola.

The earliest known fans date from the 1890s. They were made of cardboard with attached wooden handles. They typically carried the same medicinal claims that appeared on other Coca-Cola advertising from the time. From the late 1890s and well into the 1910s, the Company used "Japanese" rice paper fans with bamboo handles. After that time, cardboard fans were distributed. Fans were given away to individuals, as well as to churches and other civic organizations. Their value as an advertising device is at once clear. As an individual was suffering from the heat of a long, hot summer, what better time to remind him or her of the cooling effects of an ice-cold glass or bottle of

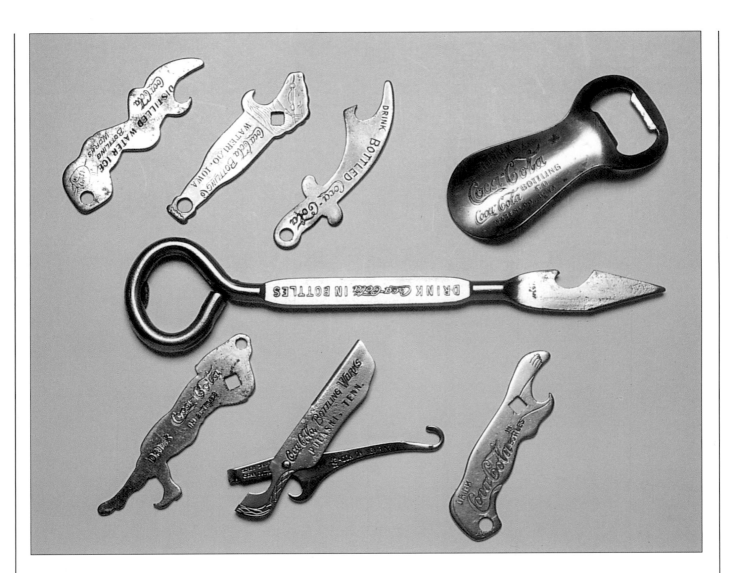

ABOVE **Metal openers, c. 1905 to c. 1925, 7 × 20 cm (2¾ to 7¾ inches) long.** As seen in this photograph, bottle openers were produced in a variety of shapes and sizes.

RIGHT **Rice-paper fan, c. 1900, 25 × 38 cm (10 × 15 inches).** Although the construction of this fan is typical of those from the early 1900s, the artwork on this example with its spider, web, dragonfly and other insects is quite unusual.

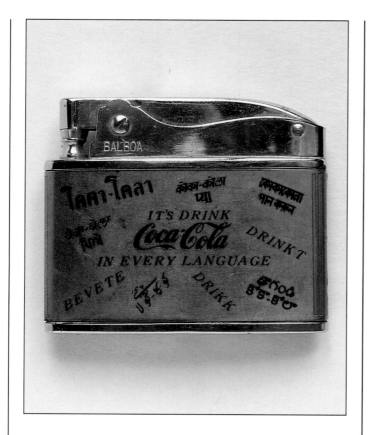

ABOVE **Metal pocket lighter, c. 1955, 5 × 4 cm (2⅛ × 1¾ inches). To celebrate its worldwide appeal, The Coca-Cola Company occasionally distributed novelties with "Drink Coca-Cola" in many languages.**

RIGHT **Table lighter, c. 1960, 11 cm (4¼ inches) high. Intended for use in homes and offices, this attractive lighter seems to be saying, "Have a Coke and a smoke".**

Coca-Cola? Charles Howard Candler, son of Company founder Asa Candler, once explained that when he was to distribute one hundred boxes of rice paper fans in Kansas City, he strung a quantity of them on a cord around his neck, and then went floor by floor, building after building, doling them out. One of the few sets of records to mention such quantities indicates that one million fans were given away in 1913 alone.

Perhaps the most enduring novelty of all, bottle openers were virtually indestructible. Usually stamped from a flat sheet of metal, they were easily and cheaply produced. To add to their appeal, some bottle openers were figural in shape, while still others had added features such as a buttonhook or shoe horn. Because individual bottlers usually arranged for the manufacture of openers, there are countless different examples available to collectors.

When sales of Coca-Cola did not increase in 1908 nearly as much as they had in 1907, Frank Robinson, secretary of The Coca-Cola Company, blamed the decreased distribution of novelties in 1908: "You may save

£6,666 ($10,000) in the advertising account by discontinuing the use of novelties, but to make this saving you may make the sales for the year one hundred thousand gallons (379,000 *l*) less than they otherwise would be". In addition to the novelties already mentioned, ice picks, fly swatters, key rings, thimbles, salt and pepper shakers, cigarette lighters, mechanical pencils, pens, ashtrays, scorekeepers, sheet music, jewellery, advertising buttons and sewing kits have all been used at one time or another to promote Coca-Cola. Novelties were distributed to consumers by door-to-door canvassing, through mass mailings, as souvenirs of bottling plant tours, for redemption of bottle caps and by mail-in offers, to name a few methods.

Although of minimal cost, a novelty given to the right person could have a long-lasting effect. The intrinsic value of such items explains why so many have survived.

BELOW **Metal spinner, c. 1900, 7 cm (2¾ inches) long. When friends gathered around a soda fountain table, they could use this hand-shaped, lithographed tin spinner to determine who paid next.**

BELOW **Metal badge, 1916, 7 cm (2¾ inches) long. This gold-plated convention badge and name tag, with cloisonné inserts, was given to attendees at the 1916 Coca-Cola Bottlers Convention.**

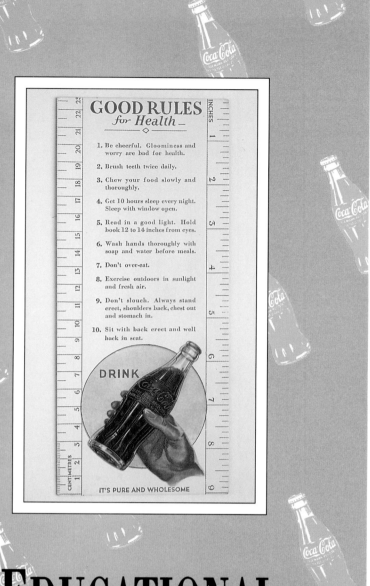

GOOD RULES
for Health

1. Be cheerful. Gloominess and worry are bad for health.

2. Brush teeth twice daily.

3. Chew your food slowly and thoroughly.

4. Get 10 hours sleep every night. Sleep with window open.

5. Read in a good light. Hold book 12 to 14 inches from eyes.

6. Wash hands thoroughly with soap and water before meals.

7. Don't over-eat.

8. Exercise outdoors in sunlight and fresh air.

9. Don't slouch. Always stand erect, shoulders back, chest out and stomach in.

10. Sit with back erect and well back in seat.

DRINK

IT'S PURE AND WHOLESOME

EDUCATIONAL MATERIALS

CHAPTER 13

When Coca-Cola was first sold, its tonic properties were advertised as being perfect for the work-weary. In light of its almost medicinal qualities, it was implicitly understood that Coca-Cola simply was not a drink for children. Because of the high caffeine content (which was nearly three times what it is now), combined with persistent, but erroneous, rumours about alcohol and cocaine, some mothers forbade their children to drink it. For its part, The Coca-Cola Company did not try to appeal to children in its early years. With very rare exceptions, Company advertising never portrayed children drinking Coca-Cola. With the passage of the Pure Food and Drug Act in 1906 and the reduction of the caffeine content in the late 1910s, The Coca-Cola Company began a slow and subtle foray into the so-called youth market in the 1920s.

Since children in the 1920s had little disposable income with which to buy 3p (5¢) servings of Coca-Cola, appealing to them directly would have been pointless. What The Coca-Cola Company and its bottlers did instead was use the educational system to reach children. They moved cautiously at first, approaching teachers, headmasters and district superintendents, rather than contacting schoolchildren directly. Educators were invited to take tours of bottling plants, and they were sent free booklets telling them how safe and wholesome Coca-Cola was. On a more significant scale, many bottlers donated utilitarian items to schools. Coca-Cola pencils, blotters and calendars, all very obviously useful, were the most popular giveaways. Many bottlers also donated clocks with Coca-Cola advertising messages. Writing in an early 1920s edition of *The Coca-Cola Bottler* magazine, one bottler boasted that he had a Coca-Cola clock hanging in every schoolroom in his territory. These initial donations and their subsequent use in the classroom opened the schoolroom door for a direct approach later.

In 1923, The Coca-Cola Company played host to the annual "Sales and Advertising Conference of the Bottlers of Coca-Cola". For the first time at that conference, it was openly suggested that advertising efforts be directed specifically towards children. Roy Booker, a spokesman

LEFT **Blotter, c. 1935, 10 × 23 cm (3⅞ × 9 inches). Besides soaking up extra ink, this Canadian blotter provided healthful hints and could also be used as a ruler.**

ABOVE **Blotter, c. 1905, 24 × 10 cm (9½ × 4 inches). A blotter is a small rectangular piece of heavy absorbent paper used for soaking up excess ink deposited by writing with a fountain pen.**

BELOW **School kit in envelope, 1935, 23 × 30 cm (9 × 11⅞ inches). For 6p (10¢), a schoolchild received a bottle of Coca-Cola along with a writing tablet, a pencil, a blotter and a ruler.**

ABOVE **Blotter, 1927, 15 × 9 cm (6⅛ × 3⅜ inches). This blotter promoting Coca-Cola in the home is typical of the artwork used to advertise Coca-Cola in the late 1920s.**

for an advertising novelties company, outlined his philosophy as follows: "And the children! My! What an opportunity for the bottler who looks ahead. The successful bottler is the man who always keeps his mind open toward tomorrow. The consumers of bottled Coca-Cola today will be increased by another group of consumers within the next ten years; and this group is in your community today attending the grammar and high schools . . . You must sell them on Coca-Cola at the time when their minds are most impressionable".

Booker proposed that bottlers "give each child a ruler, a pencil and three blotters". The total cost for these items would be a mere 2½p (4¢). If a bottler had 5,000 schoolchildren in his town, it would cost him only £133 ($200) a year. Booker predicted that if a bottler carried out this program for three years at a cost of £400 ($600), he would have "5,000 new customers, to say nothing of the immediate results". Apparently many bottlers heeded Booker's advice. Although pencils and blotters had long been standard Coca-Cola giveaways, rulers were another matter. Following Booker's presentation, the Company began producing a special ruler imprinted with the words, "Do Unto Others As You Would Have Them Do Unto You". This Golden Rule ruler had possibly the longest life of any advertising item for Coca-Cola — it remained virtually unchanged for more than forty-five years.

ABOVE **Booklet, 1928, 19 × 13 cm (7½ × 5¼ inches). To help children learn the alphabet, each page of this full-colour "ABC Booklet" has a poem about a letter of the alphabet.**

ABOVE **Cards, 1923, 5 × 8 cm (2⅛ × 3⅛ inches). In 1923, Coca-Cola bottlers began distributing sets of "Nature Study" cards to educate children about the world around them.**

The list of Coca-Cola advertising materials given away free to schoolchildren soon expanded to include not just rulers, pencils and blotters, but rubbers, tablets, book covers, pens, maps and printed schedules for school athletic events. Coca-Cola bottlers also distributed materials with more substantial educational value. In the late 1920s and 1930s, "Nature Study" cards described the natural world; in the early 1930s, "Famous Doctors" folders detailed significant medical advancements over the centuries; in the 1940s and 1950s, "Our America" kits described major American industries; in the late 1950s and early 1960s, "Elementary Science Laboratory" kits enabled students to conduct their own modest scientific experiments; and in the late 1960s, "Golden Legacy" comic books told the history of famous black Americans. The "Black Guardians of Freedom" materials that complemented the Golden Legacy series included an excerpt from Martin Luther King's "I Have a Dream" speech and concluded with the statement that "no man can be free until all men are free". Clearly, such educational advertising materials did more than sell a soft drink. They celebrated and reinforced the best attributes of the people and culture where Coca-Cola was sold.

LEFT **Plastic inkwell and box, 1948, 10 × 10 × 9 cm (3¾ × 3¾ × 3⅛ inches). Before ballpoint pens, everyone used fountain pens or dipping pens which needed to have their ink replenished from inkwells such as this one.**

RIGHT **Mechanical pencil, 1942, 15 cm (5⅞ inches) long. The miniature bottle on the end of this mechanical lead pencil is actually filled with Coca-Cola.**

BELOW **Paper book cover, c. 1956, 51 × 30 cm (20 × 12 inches). Since the 1920s, Coca-Cola bottlers have distributed millions of book covers to schools. This one shows US President Eisenhower.**

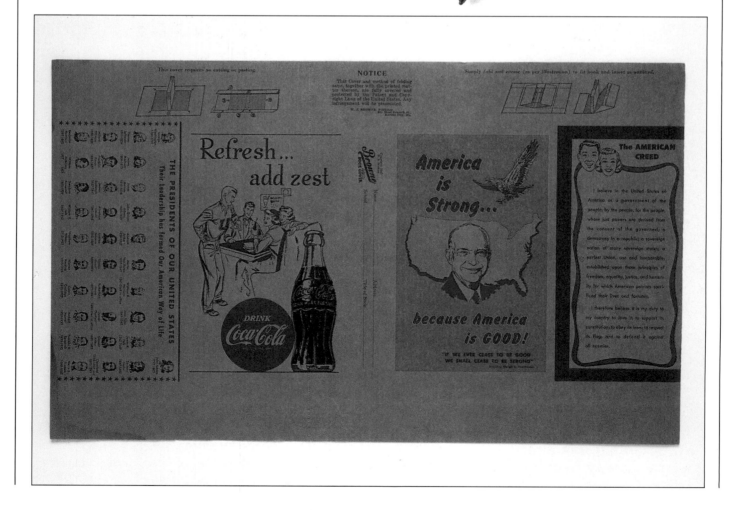

Because they were given out in such large quantities, these educational items are readily available for today's collectors. Additionally, since the same kinds of items were distributed over several decades, it is sometimes difficult to date them correctly. The advertising slogans printed on these items can frequently be used to pinpoint the years of use more accurately. For example, "Pure As Sunlight" was first used in the late 1920s and continued into the 1930s; "A Pure Drink of Natural Flavors" was used in the 1930s; "Coke = Coca-Cola" was used in the 1940s and 1950s; "things go better with Coke" and "It's the real thing" appeared in the 1960s; and "Have a Coke and smile", "Coke adds life" and "Coke is it!" in the 1970s. However, since some items were issued year after year with the same slogans, such as "Drink Coca-Cola in Bottles", "Drink Coca-Cola Refreshing" and "Have a Coke," it is nearly impossible to tell exactly when individual examples were actually given out.

ABOVE **Cardboard map, c. 1955, 61 × 47 cm (24 × 18½ inches). With its distances between major US cities, this wall map could have been used in schools as well as petrol stations.**

MISCELLANEOUS ITEMS

CHAPTER 14

For a variety of reasons, there are Coca-Cola collectibles that don't fit conveniently into any of the previous chapters. For example, one category of miscellaneous items consists of those things used to conduct the mundane business of manufacturing, distributing and selling Coca-Cola. Special awards and trophies form another such category. Advertising specialties offered only once, or at most a few times, constitute yet another group of miscellaneous items. Finally, there are some items that were not produced by The Coca-Cola Company or its bottlers, but which nevertheless show advertising for Coca-Cola.

In order to conduct the affairs of any large business, certain items are necessary. For example, stationery, invoices, receipts and cheques are used in normal everyday business operations. When such items carry the Coca-Cola trademark, they become instantly collectible. Ordinary building hardware, such as doorknobs and padlocks, when used in Coca-Cola office buildings and plants, was sometimes marked with the Coca-Cola logo. Today the disposable plastic seals on syrup containers are similarly marked. Although these items would ordinarily go unnoticed, the inclusion of the Coca-Cola trademark renders them collectible.

To honour significant achievements, businesses have traditionally given awards to their employees. The Coca-Cola Company and its bottlers adhered to this practice. For example, they gave jewellery to employees to recognize such achievements as the number of years of employment, safe driving and retirement. In addition, The Coca-Cola Company presented plaques and awards to individual bottlers in order to acknowledge high sales figures or to celebrate bottlers' anniversaries.

Over the years, in an effort to increase their own business, manufacturers of advertising items have presented the Company and its bottlers with new ideas for promoting Coca-Cola. Some of the resulting items were adopted and issued over long periods of time, while others were tried for a year or two and then discontinued because

LEFT **Plaque, 1953, 46 × 18 cm (18 × 7¼ inches). The bottler in Newcastle, Indiana, was presented with this "per capita" award for selling 200 bottles of Coca-Cola to each man, woman and child in his territory in the year 1953.**

of their expense or inferior design. This group of short-lived items includes some of the most desirable of all Coca-Cola collectibles.

Not only has the Coca-Cola trademark been used to promote the sale of Coca-Cola, it has also been used by other firms to advertise their own products. Many manufacturers of advertising material have used Coca-Cola items made by them as exemplars of the quality of their work. For example, advertisements for sign makers often showed a Coca-Cola sign among others, and truck manufacturers frequently pictured Coca-Cola trucks in their advertising. The message was clear: If these items were good enough for The Coca-Cola Company, they were good enough for other businesses as well. Vintage picture postcards and photographs showing Coca-Cola items also fall into this category.

LEFT **Metal doorknobs, c. 1915, 5 cm (2⅛-inch) diameter. As The Coca-Cola Company built branch offices throughout the United States, they equipped them with brass door knobs such as the ones shown here from the Candler Building in Baltimore, Maryland.**

BELOW **Plaque, 1953, 46 × 36 cm (18 × 14 inches). During the 1950s, many bottlers reached their fiftieth year in business. In recognition of this accomplishment, they were presented with bronze and walnut plaques such as the one shown here.**

ABOVE **Charm, 1961, 3 × 4 cm (1¼ × 1⅝ inches).** When a bottler had bought enough Coca-Cola syrup, he was inducted into "The 100 Thousand Gallon Club" and presented with this diamond-studded gold memento.

RIGHT **Bakelite radio, 1933, 59 cm (23¼ inches) high.** At a cost of £12.50 ($18.75) each, the "Bottle Radio" was one of the most expensive advertising items presented to retailers during the Great Depression.

LEFT **Wooden bench, c. 1920, 120 cm (47½ inches).** Manufactured by the Hackney Wagon Company of Wilson, North Carolina, this bench would have been placed in front of a shop or petrol station where bottled Coca-Cola was sold.

ABOVE **Wall planters, 1932, each 30 cm (12 inches) high. Made of moulded chipboard and containing paper flowers, this planter set was designed for upscale outlets such as cinemas.**

LEFT **Electric toaster, c. 1930, 20 cm (7¾-inch) diameter. After they had been made, sandwiches were put into this appliance in order to toast the Coca-Cola trademark onto the bread.**

LEFT **Metal string holder, 1939, 32 × 39 × 18 cm (12⅝ × 15⅝ × 6⅞ inches). In the days when shop purchases were routinely wrapped in paper and tied with string, this string dispenser hanging over the counter would have been much appreciated by the shop owner.**

ABOVE **Metal and Bakelite ashtray, 1938, 18 cm (7¼ inches) high. This ashtray was called a "Pullmatch", because when a match was pulled from the holder atop the bottle, it was automatically ignited.**

LEFT **Bakelite match dispenser, 1934, 30 cm (12⅛ inches) high. Since Coca-Cola and cigarettes were often sold at the same establishments, Coca-Cola bottlers saw the opportunity to provide retailers with an advertising item that was both useful and long-lasting.**

LEFT **Plastic mileage meter,
c. 1950, 18 cm (7 inches) high. By
spinning the printed drum inside
this particular mileage meter, a
motorist could determine how
far it was from Martinsville,
Virginia, to cities in Virginia and
nearby states.**

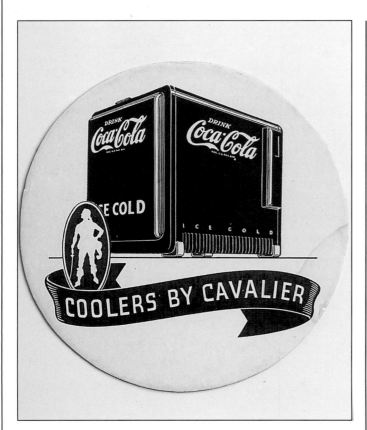

ABOVE **Cardboard coaster,
c. 1940, 10 cm (3⅞-inch)
diameter. These coasters are
examples of advertising items**
distributed by **manufacturers of
merchandising items that
advertise not only their
products, but Coca-Cola as well.**

ABOVE **Metal coaster, c. 1953,
10 cm (3½-inch) diameter.**

REPRODUCTION, FANTASY AND LICENSED ITEMS

The 1970s saw The Coca-Cola Company's first real interest in the memorabilia craze that had begun sweeping the nation. The Company offered reproductions of early trays, calendars, glasses and other items to a nostalgia-hungry public. The ensuing interest generated by these reproductions is largely responsible for launching the Coca-Cola memorabilia collecting phenomenon which continues to this day. All this collecting activity also attracted unscrupulous individuals who, without the permission of The Coca-Cola Company, produced fake advertising pieces marked with the Coca-Cola trademark; and the wholesale manufacture of large quantities of illegal collectibles flourished during the 1970s. Long after these bogus items were produced, they continue to cause problems for novice and experienced collectors alike. Unfortunately, the more age these fraudulent pieces acquire, the more difficult it is to convince some collectors that they are fakes.

Technically speaking, a reproduction is a copy of an older item. At first glance, the casual observer may not notice any discernible difference between the two. However, upon closer inspection, a knowledgeable collector will always be able to detect differences between the original and the reproduction. For example, today's printing processes are different from those used at the turn of the century. The quality of workmanship is rarely as good on a reproduction as on an original. There are often subtle variations in size colour, and material between the two. If a collector has the opportunity to place a reproduction and its original counterpart side by side, the differences are usually strikingly obvious. Unfortunately, collectors rarely have this advantage when they are about to make a purchase. Among the most common reproductions are trays, signs, calendars, watch fobs, pocketknives and pocket mirrors.

A fantasy item is one that appears to be old, but in reality is not. Unlike a reproduction, a fantasy item has no original counterpart. To give them an air of authenticity, most fantasy items incorporate old artwork and slogans as part of their design. Some even include bogus dates, manufacturers and events in order to mislead the unwary.

LEFT **Cardboard sign, 1973, 47 × 58 cm (18⅜ × 23 inches). Shown here is the advertising used by The Coca-Cola Company for the** **first set of three reproduction trays that were offered for sale in the United States in 1973.**

LEFT **Tray, 1923, 27 × 34 cm (10⅜ × 13¼ inches), and 1974 reproduction, 32 × 38 cm (12⅜ × 15⅛ inches). Even though the Company used a different shape from the original (left), the reproduction tray (right) is still mistaken today for an old tray because of the antique-style artwork.**

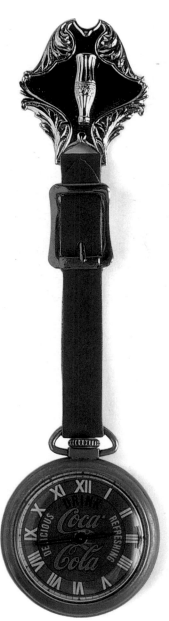

ABOVE **Pocket mirror, 1920 and 1973 reproduction, both 4 × 7 cm (1¾ × 2¾ inches). A side-by-side comparison of an original pocket** mirror (left) with a reproduction (right) accentuates the richer colours and finer detail of the original.

RIGHT **Fantasy pocket watch and fob, c. 1972, 19 cm (7½ inches) long. This pocket watch is authentically old, but the new face was added in more recent times. The attached silver watch fob and strap are entirely new.**

RIGHT **Calendar, 1974, 29 × 55 cm (11½ × 21½ inches). The Company's annual calendar for 1974 carried reprints of six calendar girls from the 1920s. Trimmed and framed, these prints have sometimes been passed off as originals.**

ABOVE **Commemorative tray, 1982, 33 × 27 cm (13 × 10⅝ inches). Recent trays manufactured for the collectors' market occasionally feature** artwork that no one would mistake as old. Some trays, such as this one from Pembroke, Florida, claim to be limited editions to enhance their value.

ABOVE **Fantasy belt buckle, c. 1973, 10 × 6 cm (4 × 2⅝ inches). Belt buckles such as this** one made of brass and marked "Tiffany", first appeared in collectors' markets in the 1970s.

Over the years, these fantasy items have included brass belt buckles, metal free-drink tokens, so-called pub mirrors, trays, pocket mirrors, money clips, paperweights, pocketknives, playing cards, glassware, signs, watch fobs and pin-back buttons. Other fantasy items have been created by taking truly old, unmarked items and adding the Coca-Cola trademark. These items are somewhat harder to detect because the items themselves are indeed genuinely old. The list of these items includes pocketknives, pocket watches, watch fobs, bone-handled cutlery, celluloid dresser sets, glass door knobs and straight razors.

In the mid-1980s, The Coca-Cola Company established a licensing programme whereby it officially sanctioned the manufacture of items bearing the Coca-Cola trademark. Although many such items feature old Coca-Cola advertising artwork, they are not meant to fool anyone into thinking they are genuinely old. Licensed items include clothing, towels, rugs, watches, playing and collectors cards, postcards, trays, glassware, pins, napkin and straw dispensers, commemorative bottles, Christmas ornaments, calendars, limited edition prints, puzzles, canisters and thermometers.

ABOVE **Fantasy tokens, c. 1975, 3 cm (1⅛ inches) square, 3 cm (1¼ inches) square, 4 × 3 cm (1½ × 1 inches). Although they often carry early dates from the 1910s, these "tokens" are fantasy items since there never were any such items originally.**

BELOW **Fantasy pocketknives, c. 1975, 6 cm (2½ inches) and 10 cm (3½ inches) long. Easily mass-produced by unscrupulous individuals, fantasy pocketknives can be found at almost any flea market.**

As even the most casual reader will have surmised by now, there are nearly as many reproduction, fantasy and licensed items as there are old surviving collectibles. New items are being produced at an ever-increasing rate. It is impossible to devise a set of rules that will permit collectors to infallibly recognize what is authentically old and what is not. However, there are a few strategies to guide collectors, particularly novices. First, the more authentic Coca-Cola collectibles a collector sees personally, the less likely he or she will be deceived by reproductions and fantasy items. Consequently, a collector should get to know other collectors and take the opportunity to study their collections. Antique advertising shows, auctions, museums and collectors' conventions are not only excellent places to meet other collectors, but to examine original items as well. Second, there are numerous reference books and price guides which picture Coca-Cola collectibles and provide additional descriptions and information.

ABOVE **Commemorative pin set in frame, 1985, 39 × 31 cm (15¼ × 12¼ inches). As the official soft drink of the National Football League, Coca-Cola issued this pin set to celebrate the American football's Super Bowl XIX.**

BELOW **Commemorative bottles, 1975, 1986 and 1993, 20 cm (7¾ inches), 25 cm (9¾ inches) and 20 cm (7¾ inches) high.**

APPENDIX

There have been a number of other books written about Coca-Cola, some of which have become collectible in their own right. Books about Coca-Cola fall into two categories: those that focus on advertising collectibles bearing the famous Coca-Cola trademark and those that focus on some aspect of the history of Coca-Cola. The book list below is separated into these two groups.

No book pictures all the known advertising of The Coca-Cola Company. Since prices vary yearly and from place to place, no price guide can be totally accurate about the values placed on Coca-Cola collectibles. The best one can hope for in a price guide is to learn what's available and to get an idea of the relative value of collectibles by comparing prices within categories. Books that concentrate on one area of specialization obviously can go into more depth than is possible in a general collectibles book. The history books are included as references for Coca-Cola collecting, because having a knowledge and appreciation of the people and times which shaped the history of Coca-Cola makes one a more knowledgeable collector of the items used to advertise the product.

You should not allow the opinion of an individual who writes a book to override your best judgment when buying. It is a mistake to buy an item solely on the advice given in a book. You should take heed of the reference books below, but then buy an item because it "speaks" to you — it strikes some resonant feelings within you. You will make some mistakes (as we all do), but you will make fewer of them in the long run if you learn to rely on your own instincts.

Also included below are museums, clubs, stores, auctions, mail-order catalogs, and appraisers which specialize in Coca-Cola advertising.

BOOKS ABOUT COCA-COLA COLLECTIBLES

BIASIO, MARIATERESA & FADINI, UGO, *Coca-Cola un mito.* Rome: Leonardo De Luca, 1992. (110 pages)

CHOLOT, GERARD, CUZON-VERRIER, DANIEL, & LEMARE, PIERRE, *Les Plus Belles Affiches de Coca-Cola.* Paris: Editions Denoël, 1986. (144 pages)

COPE, JIM, *Soda Water Advertising.* Orange, TX: author, 1971. (80 pages)

DE COURTIVRON, GAEL, *Collectible Coca-Cola Toy Trucks.* Paducah, KY: Collector Books, 1995. (240 pages)

EBNER, STEVE & WRIGHT, JEFF, *Vintage Coca-Cola Machines.* Gaithersburg, MD: Fun-tronics, 1989. (110 pages)

GOLDSTEIN, SHELLEY & HELEN, *Coca-Cola Collectibles, Vols. 1–4.* Woodland Hills, CA: authors, 1972–76. (78–88 pages each)

HILL, DEBORAH GOLDSTEIN, *Price Guide to Coca-Cola Collectibles.* Radnor, PA: Wallace-Homestead, 1991. (196 pages)

MIX, RICHARD, *The Mix Guide to Commemorative Bottles.* San Antonio, TX: Multi-Ads, 1990. (200 pages)

MUNSEY, CECIL, *The Illustrated Guide to the Collectibles of Coca-Cola.* New York: Hawthorn Books, Inc., 1972. (334 pages)

MURKEN-ALTROGGE, CHRISTA, *Coca-Cola Art: Konsum, Kult, Kunst.* München: Klinkhardt & Biermann, 1991. (208 pages)

PETRETTI, ALLAN, *Petretti's Coca-Cola Collectibles Price Guide, 9th Edition.* Hackensack, NJ: Nostalgia Publications, Inc., 1994. (500 pages)

SCHMIDT, BILL & JAN, *The Schmidt Museum Collection of Coca-Cola Memorabilia.* Elizabethtown, KY: Schmidt Books, 1983. (160 pages)

WEINBERGER, MARTY & DON, *Coca-Cola Trays from Mexico & Canada.* Willow Grove, PA: authors, 1979. (40 pages)

WILSON, AL & HELEN, *Wilson's Coca-Cola Price Guide.* Atglen, PA: Schiffer Publishing, 1994. (256 pages)

BOOKS ABOUT THE HISTORY OF COCA-COLA

ALLEN, FREDERICK, *Secret Formula: How Brilliant Marketing and Relentless Salesmanship Made Coca-Cola the Best Known Product in the World.* New York: HarperBusiness, 1994. (500 pages)

CANDLER, CHARLES HOWARD, *Asa Griggs Candler.* Atlanta: Emory University, 1950. (502 pages)

COCA-COLA COMPANY, *The Coca-Cola Company: An Illustrated Profile.* Atlanta: author, 1974. (110 pages)

DIETZ, LAWRENCE, *Soda Pop.* New York: Simon & Schuster, 1973. (184 pages)

ELLIOTT, CHARLES, *"Mr. Anonymous" Robert Woodruff of Coca-Cola.* Atlanta: Cherokee Publishing Company, 1982. (310 pages)

GRAHAM, ELIZABETH CANDLER, *The Real Ones, Four Generations of the First Family of Coca-Cola.* Fort Lee, NJ: Barricade Books, 1992. (344 pages)

Hoy, Anne, *Coca-Cola: The First 100 Years.* Atlanta: The Coca-Cola Company, 1986. (160 pages)

Kahn, E. J., *The Big Drink: The Story of Coca-Cola.* New York: Random House, 1960. (174 pages)

Louis, J. C., & Yazijian, Harvey, *The Cola Wars.* New York: Everest House, 1980. (386 pages)

Mayo, P. Randolph, *Coca-Cola Heritage: A Photographic History of the Biedenharn Coca-Cola Bottling Business.* San Antonio, TX: author, 1990. (118 pages)

Oliver, Thomas, *The Real Coke, The Real Story.* New York: Random House, 1986. (234 pages)

Patou-Senez, Julie, *Coca-Cola Story.* Paris: G. Authier, 1978. (274 pages)

Pendergrast, Mark, *For God, Country, and Coca-Cola.* New York: Scribner's, 1993. (556 pages)

Shartar, Martin & Shavin, Norman, *The Wonderful World of Coca-Cola.* Atlanta: Capricorn Corporation, 1981. (64 pages)

Staples, Bob & Charles, Barbara, *Dream of Santa: Haddon Sundblom Vision.* Washington, DC: Staples & Charles, 1992. (84 pages)

Steinbach Palazzini, Fiora, *Coca-Cola Superstar.* New York: Barron's, 1989. (142 pages)

Watters, Pat, *Coca-Cola: An Illustrated History.* Garden City, NY: Doubleday & Co., Inc., 1978. (288 pages)

USEFUL ADDRESSES

C. C. Tray-ders, 611 North 5th St., Reading, PA 19601–2201, USA. Appraisers.

Coca-Cola Collectors Club, P.O. Box 49166, Atlanta, GA 30359–1166, USA. International organization.

Coca-Cola Fifth Avenue, 711 Fifth Avenue, New York, NY 10022, USA. Coca-Cola display and store.

Memorabilia Club, Casella postale 540, 20101, Italy. Italian organization.

Muddy River Trading Company, 4803 Lange Lane, SW, Roanoke, VA 24018, USA. Auctions.

Nostalgia Publications, 21 South Lake Dr., Hackensack, NJ 07601, USA. Auctions.

Pop's Mail Order Collectibles, 4439 Hudgins, Memphis, TN 38116, USA. Catalog sales.

Schmidt Museum of Coca-Cola Memorabilia, 1201 North Dixie, Elizabethtown, KY 42702, USA. Museum and store.

Tucker Bay Company, P.O. Box 70127, Stockton, CA 95267, USA. Auctions.

U-Grade It Video Auctions, 4411 Bazetta Road, Cortland, Ohio 44410, USA. Auctions.

The World of Coca-Cola, 55 Martin Luther King, Jr., Drive, Atlanta, GA 30303, USA. Museum and store.

The authors, Bill Bateman & Randy Schaeffer, 611 North 5th Street, Reading, PA 19601, USA, Telephone 610–373–3333, look forward to hearing from fellow Coca-Cola collectors and enthusiasts. They are also interested in adding old and unusual items to their collection.

INDEX